THE MAKING OF TH

SPAWN

THE MAKING OF THE MOVIE
SPAWN

Rachel Aberly

TITAN BOOKS

SPAWN
THE MAKING OF THE MOVIE
ISBN 1 85286 839 2

Published by
Titan Books
42-44 Dolben Street
London SE1 0UP

First edition October 1997
10 9 8 7 6 5 4 3 2 1

British Library Cataloguing-in-Publication Data. A catalogue record for
this book is available from the British Library.

Design by Osmond Browne.
Production by Bob Kelly.

Spawn photographs by Peter Iovino.

> **Dedication**
> Dedicated to the memory of Morley Kolomyjec for all the
> support he gave me while he could.
> — Todd McFarlane

Acknowledgements

The Publisher would like to thank Rachel Aberly, everyone at Todd
McFarlane Productions, especially Todd McFarlane, Terry Fitzgerald,
Carmen Bryant, Wanda Kolomyjec, Sheila Egger and Julia Simmons,
everyone at New Line, especially Chris Rapp, David Imhoff and Travis
Topa, Christopher Raimo, Ellen Pasternack, and the cast and crew of
Spawn for their tireless help with this project.

Printed and bound in Great Britain by Stephens and George Ltd,
Merthyr Industrial Estate, Dowlais, Merthyr Tydfil.

CONTENTS

INTRODUCTION

or those who don't know me, I'm actually two different people melded into one. There is the boring, average husband/father, who still plays baseball and does all the things that average husbands/fathers do. Then there is the other side of me, the side that sees business negotiations as a war, who sees the person across the table from me as the enemy.

That brings us to Spawn. He is an attitude, and within that attitude is my attitude: compromise doesn't have a place in war. *Spawn* is a guy who doesn't follow tried and true formulas, who doesn't do things in a politically correct fashion. In the heat of battle, you have to use whatever means are at your disposal to get your point across, and that is the essence of what this character stands for.

Spawn is a guy who, if the system doesn't work, is willing to take things into his own hands.

History tells us a lot of things, but it's also a bit of a crutch. Instead of trying to update themselves, people can just sit back and say that this is the way it's always been done. I don't believe that. I think we should always strive to do better, always push forth, and because of this I have been in control of the character and haven't let go of him on any level.

The movie will be dark and will continue to showcase the things I think entertain the people who like Spawn. If this character gets in the hands of people who are just going to polish him up and smooth out the rough edges, then all you are going to have left is a poor man's version of Batman. And you know what? There are a hundred of those out there. What intrigues people is the fact that Spawn isn't the guy that's necessarily going to make all the right decisions, so nothing is inevitable about the outcome.

In the end, it's that edge that continues to make *Spawn* such a success.

T. McFarlane 97

*S*pawn is the film incarnation of the phenomenally popular comic created by Todd McFarlane. A reluctant, violent character, flawed and conflicted, Spawn is afflicted by rage, jealousy and doubt. His story reflects, among others, the influences of Dante, Greek mythology and the Bible. Among its many themes, the comic incorporates the iniquities and divisions in contemporary society, highlighting the stark contrast between the 'haves' and the 'have-nots'. *Spawn* also showcases one of the few African-American stars of a comic book saga. In short, Spawn is not a conventional comic book hero and his tale is not conspicuously commercial. Yet, the series has gone on to become a

This page: *The cover to* Spawn #1 *and interior scenes featuring the character's first published appearance.*

perennial top-seller, generating millions of dollars in revenues through the comic itself, as well as via a toy line, a video game and an animated series on the American cable channel HBO. Indeed, the first issue sold an unparalleled 1,700,000 copies and subsequently sold over 100,000,000 copies worldwide,

distributed in 120 countries, translated into sixteen different languages.

Raised in Calgary, Canada, McFarlane's interest in comics began in high school, but it was an ankle injury that propelled him towards it professionally.

"I discovered the world of comics during my high school days," McFarlane relates. "I spent a lot of time drawing comic book heroes, but my ultimate dream was to play professional baseball. When I began playing baseball in Calgary, a scout for the Seattle Mariners followed my progress and ultimately, he recruited me out of the college ranks to play on the Mariners' semi-pro team.

"After I graduated high school, I attended Spokane Community College and eventually accepted a baseball scholarship to Eastern Washington State University. I continued to draw comic book characters in college and ended up with a degree in graphic design, but my focus was baseball. My dream of playing in the majors ended when I broke my ankle sliding into home. After the accident, I began to submit my drawings to different comic book publishers."

McFarlane attacked the world of comics with the same zeal he had devoted to baseball, but he was not an overnight success.

"I was determined to get a job in the comic industry," he recalls. "I drew evenings and weekends while still at school and worked two part-time jobs, one of which was running a comic book shop in Spokane. I sent my portfolio out again and again. I received over 700 rejection letters."

In 1984, he finally received an offer from Marvel/ Epic Comics, "... to pencil 'Scorpio Rose', an eleven-page back-up story in *Coyote*." The company eventually 'retired' *Coyote*, but the experience led to another invitation, this time a temporary pencilling job at DC Comics where he contributed to, among others, the *Batman: Year Two* mini-series.

Soon after, McFarlane got his proverbial 'big break' with Marvel Comics. Following an acclaimed run on *The Incredible Hulk*, McFarlane turned his artistic attentions to the company's legendary web-slinging super-hero, Spider-Man.

"My career really took off when I began to do the pencils and covers on Marvel's *Amazing Spider-Man*. That was the catalyst that launched my career as a comic book artist," McFarlane says.

Although the Spider-Man character was already established, McFarlane added his own unique style to the web-slinger, "... replacing his webs, transforming his human body and adding spider-like eyes." His idiosyncratic artistry rattled his bosses. It

the character and was willing to see what I'd do with it, but he was getting pressure from above. They were saying, 'What the hell is this spaghetti webbing and why is this kid drawing big eyes and how come he's putting black in the costume?' It definitely got me in trouble and the editor-in-chief told me I had to stop doing it that way."

McFarlane ignored the warning and fans of the series embraced the singular new look, which went on to set the standard in the illustrating community, as other artists began to copy and imitate the style.

McFarlane drew *Amazing Spider-Man* for over a year, by which time he was tired of illustrating other writers' stories. Marvel created a new title called simply *Spider-Man*, which afforded McFarlane the opportunity to not only pencil and ink but also to write. His nascent effort as an author was a huge success. Shipped in September 1990, *Spider-Man* #1 went on to become the best-selling comic of all time, selling more than 2,500,000 copies.

Despite its success, McFarlane still bristled at his lack of creative control over the characters and future royalties they might produce. He found five like-minded colleagues at Marvel and the renegades conspired to start their own rival company.

"During my tenure on *Spider-Man*, I laid plans to form my own publishing company, to allow me and other artists the freedom to create our own characters and retain the rights to them," recounts McFarlane. "After speaking with several other 'hot' Marvel artists, I learned that I was not the only one frustrated by the bureaucracy and interested in making a change."

would not be the last time the independent McFarlane would find himself at odds with the comic book establishment.

"My editor, Jim Salicrup, was the best I ever worked for, because he gave me a little latitude with

In 1992, McFarlane, along with Jim Lee, Rob Liefeld, Jim Valentino, Eric Larsen and Marc Silvestri, bolted from Marvel and created Image Comics. The new company aimed to protect the artists and allow them to retain their individuality on several levels. McFarlane explains:

"The ideology behind Image Comics stressed that each artist would retain creative control over their characters and determine how or if each character would be licensed, reaping any rewards, both creatively and financially."

Under the Image banner, Spawn was born, or rather *re*-born. McFarlane had created a partial version of Spawn as a youth and resurrected the character with the formation of Image Comics:

"I had actually developed a whole bunch of characters as a kid and Spawn just happened to be the one I pulled out of my portfolio. I didn't know if it would be the right character, but I decided to spend some time working on it, to see where it would lead."

It led to a series that has already spanned over sixty issues and shows no sign of flagging. Consistently the number one best-selling comic in America, *Spawn* has generated several spin-off mini-series such as *Spawn: Bloodfeud*, *Angela* and *Violator*, as well as a new ongoing *Spawn* title, *Curse of the Spawn*. The line of *Spawn* action figures produced by McFarlane Toys continues to fly off the shelves and the franchise has been further broadened by a *Spawn* video game, an animated series, and now the movie.

It is probably no coincidence that, like McFarlane, who dared to take on the comic book industry titans, Spawn not only defies his boss Wynn, but rebels against the Devil himself.

TODD McFARLANE

From the outset, as with the comic book and all the various *Spawn*-related creations, from merchandise to the HBO animated series, Todd McFarlane was integrally involved with the movie. McFarlane points out that his primary goal was to create a comic book, but he acknowledges that *Spawn* embodies certain qualities that lend themselves well to movies:

"You can't wag the dog with the tail, but if you do a comic and it translates to other mediums, that's a bonus."

Spawn the comic consistently set record sales, which non-coincidentally also brought instant Hollywood interest, a fact not lost on the savvy McFarlane:

"A lot of Hollywood people approached me about doing *Spawn* as a movie just because it was the number one book. It was a no-brainer for those people who are paid to buy options. Hollywood is notorious for that. But most of these people hadn't done their homework, they hadn't even seen the book

and had no love for it. They figured, well, we made a comic book movie before, we made *Batman* or *Superman* or whatever. We'll just plug it into our formula. Ultimately, that was why I felt I had to maintain control of it."

Thanks to the combined efforts of director Mark

Above right: Spawn *creator Todd McFarlane.*

Below right: *Todd guests at an ice hockey match.*

During production, McFarlane visited the set occasionally, spending as much time with the grips and electricians as the stars. His goal was to "... spread the [*Spawn*] gospel and bring the family attitude [to the production]." After the film wrapped, McFarlane worked closely with the film-makers, especially during the editing process, as they honed and polished the movie, readying it for release.

While McFarlane is intrigued by the movies, he has no intention of leaving his Phoenix home and his hydra-headed *Spawn* operation for the lure of Hollywood.

"If Hollywood is a drug," theorises McFarlane, "and it's addictive, then don't go into the room."

Dippé and producer Clint Goldman, the film came in on time and on budget. Although the film-makers are renowned for their work in visual effects, *Spawn* marks their feature début as director and producer.

"A lot of people were bidding to do *Spawn*, but I felt I would rather work with 'novices'," comments McFarlane. "Not that Mark and Clint lack experience. They set the standard in terms of visual effects. But, in *Spawn*, they will receive their first full director and producer credit. I knew they were hungry. *Spawn* was as important to them as it was to me and, certainly, it was important to their careers. They also had the young, hip attitude that was right for this movie."

McFarlane adds that Dippé, Goldman and Spaz Williams were also friends of his prior to the movie and he knew they would welcome his support and feedback, something that was vital to transferring *Spawn* from book to screen:

"I thought that the bigger the movie got, the more I'd be out of the picture on some level. I'd rather have the opportunity to provide input in a positive way for the character. I see *Spawn* like a creative child and I treat him like one of my children. Therefore, the neighbours aren't going to dress my kid, they're not going to adopt him and take away visitation rights. If they get *Spawn*, they also get the Little League father with him."

STRIP TO SCREEN

The success of the *Spawn* comic naturally attracted Hollywood's attention, and McFarlane was interested, but only on his terms.

"I could have sold the rights to *Spawn* early on, without maintaining any sort of creative control over it, but I'd hate to have to say that all I'd done on the movie version was cash a cheque," McFarlane says. "It wasn't just about making a movie, it was about making the right one."

Initial talks with Columbia Pictures fell apart because McFarlane felt the studio would not afford him enough control over his creation. New Line Cinema was more obliging, making him executive producer, thereby granting McFarlane the right to

Above right: Spawn's mutating face piece, as originally conceived.

Below right: Cast, crew and creator. The Spawn dream team.

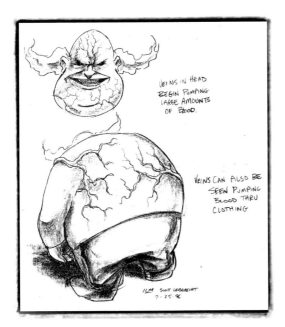

VEINS IN HEAD BEGIN PUMPING LARGE AMOUNTS OF BLOOD.

VEINS CAN ALSO BE SEEN PUMPING BLOOD THRU CLOTHING

ILM SCOTT LEBERECHT
7·25·96

"Your armour has trillions of neural connections. It is a living extension of your own instincts, instantly translating your thoughts into corresponding reality..." Every emotion Spawn feels — and in the course of the film those run the gamut from rage to despair, from jealousy to hope — triggers a corresponding physical reaction in the suit.

Spawn's sadistic guide to the abyss is a character called Clown, a perverse version of a jolly jester who occasionally mutates into other forms. His favourite transformation is his alter-ego: a giant, terrifying demon with formidable power called the Violator. The script details this process as follows: "Clown's body shakes as it grows. Pulsing as something with powerful elongated double-boned, tri-jointed limbs and razor sharp steel talons rapidly grows and takes form."

In order to bring these unique characters quite literally to life on the screen, McFarlane needed a team well-versed in visual effects. Such film-makers also had to appreciate the comic book's dark appeal and, additionally, were required to create the two universes Spawn straddles: the mortal realm and the underworld, both of which ultimately meet in the movie's climactic sequence, as Hell threatens to erupt and engulf our world.

McFarlane found the perfect artists for the movie in director Mark Dippé, visual effects supervisor and second unit director Steve "Spaz" Williams and producer Clint Goldman, all expatriates of the famed effects house, Industrial Light & Magic. Dippé and Williams created much of the eye-popping magic that made ILM famous, from the morphing process

Left: *Clown does the 'shake and pulse', courtesy of an early design sketch.*

Below: *Spawn's eye-watering 'crotch defence'.*

replace both the director and the screenwriter and veto any casting decisions. The company also conceded the film's merchandising rights to McFarlane, who promises not to sanction *Spawn* toothpaste.

Hollywood's interest in *Spawn* is not surprising, even beyond the lure of potential financial gains. The *Spawn* comic features incredibly visual, almost three-dimensional, computer-driven colour work. Coupled with the kinetic, mutating forms and the distinctive look of several *Spawn* protagonists, the series seems a natural for motion pictures. Specifically, Spawn is endowed with a living suit; as Cogliostro explains to him in the screenplay:

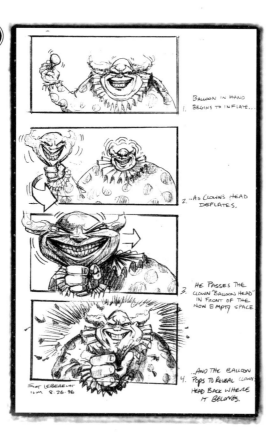

Right: *An unused storyboard sequence from Cyan's birthday party. Don't try this at home, kids!*

Below: *McFarlane and Dippé pose with John Leguizamo and Michael Jai White.*

in *Terminator 2: Judgment Day* to the mesmerising, tactile water creatures in *The Abyss*, to the dinosaurs in *Jurassic Park*, and Goldman supervised the visual effects behind Jim Carrey's elastic green face in *The Mask*. Like McFarlane, Dippé and Williams became increasingly frustrated by their lack of artistic control over the characters and ground-breaking effects they'd created, which led them to form a direct-

ing/producing partnership.

"We came up with the innovations and the art, but we weren't allowed to put our true signature on our work," Williams says. "With *Spawn*, I can finally place my digital actors in a play that I like, that I have some real involvement with. We control the stage and shape it every step of the way."

In the trio of Dippé, Williams and Goldman, McFarlane found kindred spirits. "For the movie version of *Spawn*," McFarlane says, "I needed to collaborate with people I could really trust with my ideas and characters. I felt I could do that with these guys."

McFarlane and the ILM effects maestros met soon after the *Spawn* comic book's extraordinary début. About this time, Dippé and Goldman consolidated their partnership, hoping to produce an effects-filled film independent of ILM, full of the kinds of "... fantastic characters and fantasmagoric images that I had been working on in several films," Dippé explains.

"Coincidentally, at that time, we met Todd McFarlane, who had just brought *Spawn* out to the public and he was interested in making a feature based on his characters," Dippé continues. "Of course, as soon as I read the first few books, I saw the potential of the characters and I enthusiastically jumped aboard. I wrote a story with Todd, which formed the basis of the project and it went very quickly from there. Initially, I'd just wanted to help him because I liked the book, and Todd's graphic style and storytelling were the best. I liked Todd's attitude, who he is, what he is doing. He is a very talented, bright guy. So, I gave him a few ideas and a month later, he said, 'You make the movie. Here, it's yours.'"

When the Columbia deal disintegrated, Goldman, working at that time on *The Mask* for New Line, and Dippé promised to pitch *Spawn* to New Line's president Mike DeLuca. Young, brash and unconventional, DeLuca is known for his street-smarts and cutting-edge vision.

"Actually, Mike DeLuca knew about *Spawn* when nobody else did because it was brand-new," Dippé recalls. "He said, '*Spawn*?! That's the hottest comic book around.' He knew even then, before most people had heard of the book, so in that sense he was really with us. It went from there, basically."

This story became a screenplay through the efforts of Dippé and Alan McElroy, who also scripted much of the HBO animated series and McFarlane's new *Spawn* comic book series *Curse of the Spawn*. McElroy appealed to McFarlane because he implicitly understand Spawn's emotional complexity.

"Alan seemed to really get the different layers of Spawn," McFarlane says. "He understood the con-cept of the character... that he is a government-trained, ex-assassin, so he is not going to speak the Queen's English. He's a twenty-eight year-old punk with a chip on his shoulder and he's been given a lot of power. Sometimes, he is tempted to abuse that power and occasionally he does. All the little nuances that make up who Spawn is, Alan seemed to tap into that very fast."

Indeed, it was those dark and shifting nuances that drew McElroy to the character:

"I loved that Spawn is a guy who is steeped in all this darkness but also has lightness to him. He went to Hell and back and he has all these dark powers, but deep within his soul is this moral core. He won't be forced to do things that go against what he believes in, no matter what. The fact that he is surrounded and consumed by darkness, yet he fights it and turns it to his advantage, really intrigued me. I don't know why I relate to that, but I definitely have an affinity for the character."

Below: *The film-makers kept their movie designs faithful to McFarlane's original character.*

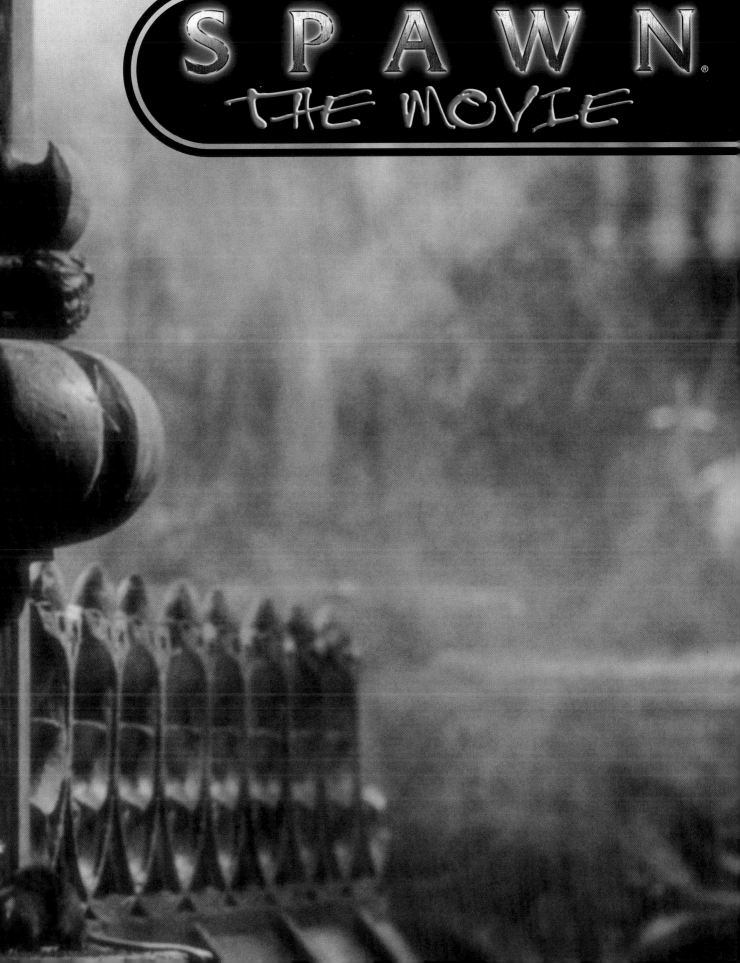

MARK DIPPÉ

Spawn represents Mark Dippé's directorial début, but by no means is it his first foray into the movie world. With interests ranging from mathematics, in which he has a degree, to music, multimedia performance and art, Dippé eventually joined Industrial Light & Magic in 1988. During the following eight years, Dippé played a pivotal part in the creation and implementation of breakthrough computer-based visual effects. His work brought 'morphing' into the popular lexicon and established computer graphic imagery as a film-making axiom. His stunning visual creations graced such films as *The Abyss, Terminator 2: Judgement Day* and *Jurassic Park*, all of which earned Academy Awards for Best Achievement in Visual Effects. His talents have also enhanced features like *Congo, The Flintstones, Rising Sun, Arachnophobia, Ghost, The Hunt for Red October* and *Back to the Future Part II*.

A film as indebted to digital wizardry as *Spawn* required a director well versed in the technology.

Producer Clint Goldman points out that while Dippé obviously brings an infinite well of digital knowledge to *Spawn*, he also possesses other attributes: "Mark is unusual in that he knows how to use the digital tools but he's also extremely literate. He understands story and character and he's got great people skills."

Dippé also had a great affection for Spawn's dark and ambiguous nature:

"His soul is on the edge. To me, the basic theme is the struggle of this man to save his soul in the face of the complex cruelty of life. Al Simmons, government agent, killing the bad guys because someone's got to do it. But when you're involved with that, your soul gets a little torn. While the tone of the film is not as grisly as the comic book, it is challenging. We wanted to remain as true to the comic book's strong graphic style and dark, ambivalent tone, but when you adapt anything, there's always going to be differences. I think that most of the fans of the book will like it, though."

Right: Director Mark Dippé and John Leguizamo on the Spawn set.

Below: *With Michael Jai White.*

Dippé calls Spawn "the classic ambiguous hero", an anti-hero defined by contradiction, a good man who lives with evil, a character whose volatile emotions materialise, chameleon-like, in the form of a living suit. All of these Spawn qualities convinced Dippé that this movie was a particularly appropriate arena for his digital expertise.

"The thing about translating a comic book to screen," explains Dippé, "is that it is ultimately a fantasy and you can break or expand some of the rules to convey that. Computer technology is particularly well suited to that kind of imagery, especially when you have characters that transform into other beings and living suits of armour that have physical responses to emotions and situations."

Moreover, Dippé adds, because the computer affords the artist the opportunity to mould and manipulate entirely invented characters and settings with relative ease, it offers "much more aesthetic freedom than traditional methods of filmmaking." In the case of *Spawn*, sometimes that even meant creating something out of nothing.

Even the cleverest computer artist might be stymied by such a situation. "The computer is just like clay — you can't do [stuff] with it unless you know how to use it," Dippé notes. Since Dippé invented some of the technologies that drive contemporary computer-based cinema, his "clay" becomes an amazing work of art, often in defiance of conventional wisdom. Many cinematic computer 'experts' will loftily assert that it is impossible to

computer-generate something as organic and random as fire in digital form, let alone an entirely unstable inferno that forms a primary setting like Hell. Quietly confident, Dippé just smiles. He's invented the impossible before. 💀

Subsequent to adapting the comic book into the eponymous movie, screenwriter Alan McElroy had become something of a *Spawn* expert. Impressed by McElroy's appreciation of the book's tone and characters, Todd McFarlane hired him to write much of the *Spawn* animated HBO series as well as the new *Spawn* title, *Curse of the Spawn*.

A precious endorsement indeed, considering Mc-Farlane's sceptical view of would-be *Spawn* writers:

"Some writers come in with the attitude, 'OK, I'm just going to rent this character.' They don't really get into all the different layers of *Spawn* and what

it's about. Alan understood the shades and textures and was really able to convey them."

McElroy became familiar with the comic prior to his involvement, when a friend, interested in pursuing the movie rights, recommended it to him.

"I'm not a comic book reader by any means," says McElroy, "but I picked it up and was immediately hooked. It was great on all levels: the artwork, the stories, the characters. It was incredibly interesting."

The comic's plot, characters and themes contained an uncanny resemblance to a script McElroy had written, entitled *Bat Out of Hell*: "That script was about a guy who escapes Hell and is chased by

Right: *Screenplay writer Alan McElroy.*

clown-like bounty hunters. The attitude and tone of the script were incredibly close to *Spawn*."

Apparently, Mark Dippé was familiar with McElroy's script and the similarity between it and *Spawn* struck him too. Dippé and Goldman approached McElroy about potentially penning the movie.

In writing the film, McElroy says he "stayed pretty close to the original material. All the main characters are there; the story is as it appears in the comic book, in terms of the issue of Al Simmons' murder and going to Hell and returning five years later. All that is in the film."

More to the point, McElroy says, the film echoes the book's underlying themes. To McElroy, those themes are at the heart of *Spawn* and a major source of its appeal:

"A comic book is obviously episodic and I had to condense it into a movie. Essentially, I looked at what it was about thematically. On a spiritual level, what does Spawn have to face? His ethics, his morality, even his own humanity become incredible dilemmas for him. The appeal of the comic is the human issues it explores — love, death, betrayal, revenge and the nature of good and evil as it relates to a man's soul. Spawn deals with real and basic feelings that we all relate to."

McElroy worked closely with Mark Dippé to tailor a script that would also showcase the incredible effects for which the director was renowned.

"Mark had a definite idea of what he wanted to see," explains McElroy, "and because he is such an effects expert, he knew what could be done and what couldn't. That made my job a lot easier. We talked about the story for months. He would suggest certain sequences and events and I would structure them logically."

McElroy's empathy for *Spawn* reveals his interest in psychology. He received a degree in the subject from Miami University. McElroy also attended school in Boston and Luxembourg. Eventually, he moved to Los Angeles, where he published his first short story, a horror tale called *The Dead Thing*. He segued into screenwriting, for both television and movies. His credits include *Halloween 4: The Return of Michael Myers*, *Rapid Fire*, *Murder by Night* and *Wheels of Terror*. McElroy also directed the short film *Under the Car* for American cable channel Showtime.

SPAWN / AL SIMMONS

S pawn is the undead *doppelgänger* of covert agent Al Simmons. In life, Simmons was a highly-trained assassin and expert executor of clandestine, dangerous and often amoral government operations. The increasingly ruthless and indiscriminate assignments handed out by his boss Jason Wynn began to chafe Simmons. This, coupled with the love he felt for his girlfriend Wanda and her pleas for him to leave the business of death for good, finally convinced Simmons to tell Wynn he was to quit after his next assignment. In truth, this mission would be his last action as Al Simmons.

Deceived and trapped by Wynn and the lethal Jessica Priest, Simmons dies a terrible death, incinerated in a hellish blaze.

Death does not exactly destroy Simmons. He returns, grotesquely resurrected, as a powerful, disfigured creature called Spawn, the appointed leader of an Army of Darkness, the unwilling instrument

of Armageddon. Spawn struggles both to master his new-found abilities and escape his infernal fate.

Both roles were incarnated by Michael Jai White. Prior to pursuing his career in acting, White taught juvenile delinquents and emotionally-disturbed children. While he no longer teaches, he still strives to reach children and hopes that this troubled anti-hero, Spawn, will help him to do so: "Spawn is a flawed character but he works through [his flaws] to become a better person, which is a great message for kids."

He adds that *Spawn* may appeal to a broader audience as well: "I think it has the unique possibility of being perceived different ways by a diversity of people. There are great visual effects in the film and people who just want to escape will find satisfaction. Yet, it's a bittersweet, almost

JUST SQUEEZE...

Shakespearean story. Those people who are searching for something deeper will find that too."

Raised in the mean section of Bridgeport, Connecticut, White describes himself as a shy youth, the youngest of four children, and an easy target. He found a means of defence through karate. Like the living suit that protects Spawn, karate became White's armour, and, like Spawn, White learned that his mind and spirit were deeply connected to his new-found physical skills:

"When I first got into karate, it was purely for self-defence. I wanted to build an armour that could shield my sensitive nature from all that could harm me. I became a deeper martial artist when I realised there was more to it than just physical force. I started to develop my heart and my soul and that's when things began to click for me."

White's yin/yang approach to conserving his strength and using it at the appropriate moment paralleled Spawn's own finite supply of power that must be hoarded to avert death. It also helped him endure gruelling sessions in full prosthetic make-up.

"I saw it as an exercise in will," White explains. "In karate, the best lesson you'll ever learn is that when you physically pit yourself against something and you forge forward, it is your mind and your will that become stronger and stronger. I used that concept in this role."

This stoic attitude, director Dippé points out, is very "Spawnlike" and, indeed, White possessed several of the hero's attributes and personality traits.

"Michael is a very gifted young actor," says Dippé. "Dramatically, emotionally and intellectually, he is amazing. One of the things he brought to Spawn that was special was the way he reacts to things physically. There was something about his bearing... Spawn is not a very talkative guy. He just makes a certain move or gesture and everyone backs away. He has an incredible physical presence and Michael captured that essence. I think there was maybe an element of Spawn in Michael too, a bit of the tortured soul."

White is probably best known for his bravura portrayal of the embattled, controversial heavy-weight boxing champion Mike Tyson in the HBO telefilm *Tyson*. He also recently co-starred in John Irvin's urban drama *City of Industry*, alongside Stephen Dorff and Harvey Keitel. Other film credits include *2 Days in the Valley*, *Ring of Fire*, *Universal Soldier*, *True Identity*, *Teenage Mutant Ninja Turtles II*, *Prototype* and *Cadillac Man*. On television, he has been a series regular on the CBS show *Shaughnessy* and appeared in such series as *JAG*, *NYPD Blue*, *Martin* and *Living Single*. White top-lined in the CBS Movie-of-the-Week *The John Mink Story*, while his many stage credits include *To Kill a Mockingbird*, *The River Niger*, *The Dutchman*, *Larry the Lobster*, *La Ronde*, *Anything Goes* and *Raisin in the Sun*. 💀

TERRY/ WANDA/CYAN

Wanda Blake's hopes of building a future with Al Simmons are destroyed by his untimely and strange death. She finds comfort in Terry Fitzgerald, Al Simmons' comrade-in-arms and best friend. The two eventually fall in love, marry and have a daughter, Cyan. Wanda rebuilds her life working on behalf of children's charities and Terry trades his spying for public relations, defending and spinning Jason Wynn's odious operations. When Simmons reappears as Spawn, Fitzgerald learns the depth of Wynn's treachery and exposes him to the press, a move which nearly costs him and his family their lives.

The roles of Terry Fitzgerald and Wanda Blake were essayed by D.B. Sweeney and Theresa Randle.

Sweeney learned of the movie while working with *Spawn* producer Clint Goldman. Goldman was overseeing the alien effects for *Fire in the Sky* at Industrial Light & Magic at the same time *Spawn* director Mark Dippé and animation director Steve Williams were working on *Jurassic Park*. Sweeney explains: "I got to know them pretty well and they told me about this *Spawn* project they were developing and they said they hoped I could help them out somehow."

Sweeney's other films include *Hear No Evil*, *Roommates*, *The Cutting Edge*, *Memphis Belle*, *Eight Men Out*, *Gardens of Stone* and *Power*. On television, he recently starred in the Fox series *Strange Luck* and was featured in the acclaimed mini-series *Lonesome Dove*.

The powerful love between Al Simmons and Wanda Blake fascinated Theresa Randle and drew her to the part of Wanda. She points out that, as well as an action movie, *Spawn* is also an incredible love story, albeit an unconventional one:

"The underlying theme that Wanda and Al Simmons and Spawn really emphasise is that love never dies. She feels him constantly, even when she thinks he's dead. So, throughout the comic book and the film, Wanda is trying to figure out whether or not she's crazy, if her feelings are real, if he is really there."

Born and raised in South Central, Los Angeles, Randle starred in several movies prior to *Spawn*, including the Spike Lee films *Girl 6*, *Jungle Fever* and *Malcolm X*. She also recently appeared opposite Michael Jordan and several animated actors in *Space Jam*. An accomplished dancer, Randle is trained in several disciplines, including ballet, jazz, modern and East Indian dance.

Randle spent much of the movie with Sydney Beaudoin, who made her feature début in *Spawn* as Wanda's daughter Cyan, the little girl who is drawn to Spawn, despite his fearsome visage. Randle developed a genuine maternal affection and admiration for her on-screen daughter: "She was so sweet and unaffected, because it was her first film. So, she was a perfect Cyan. And she implicitly understood what she was doing."

The Characters

COGLIOSTRO

N icol Williamson plays Cogliostro, Spawn's mysterious tutor and guide. An immortal like Spawn, he was born as Count Alessandro di Cogliostro. At least 500 years old, Cogliostro possesses the magic and knowledge of the ancients and is committed to the destruction of Malebolgia and his ranks. He has been searching the ages for a successor and believes he has found him in Spawn. Cogliostro teaches Spawn both the breadth and limitations of his arcane powers, and helps him reconcile his conflicted soul.

Thanks to Williamson's much acclaimed portrayal of Merlin in John Boorman's epic big screen retelling of the Arthurian legend, *Excalibur*, he was no stranger to playing enigmatic mystics. When the time came to cast the role of Cogliostro, Williamson's pedigree made him the ideal choice.

However, any danger of typecasting is more than offset by the sheer range of Williamson's past performances on both stage and screen.

His much-honoured career began with the Dundee Repertory Theatre, and from there he moved on to the Royal Shakespeare Company. His performance in the play *Inadmissible Evidence* earned him the first of two British Drama Awards and led to his Broadway début in the same play.

A film version followed, in which Williamson starred, and subsequently he featured in *The Reckoning*, *The Bofors Gun* and *Laughter in the Dark*. Williamson has since co-starred with Sidney Poitier and Michael Caine in *The Wilby Conspiracy*, and played a cocaine-addicted Sherlock Holmes in *The Seven Percent Solution*. He also recently appeared in Terry Jones' *The Wind-in-the-Willows*. In addition to acting, Williamson has directed several productions at Stratford-on-Avon, as well as on Broadway, and written a novel entitled *Ming's Kingdom*. 💀

ZACK WEBB

iko Hughes plays Zack, the wily, scavenging, good-hearted street urchin who befriends Spawn and Spaz, Al Simmons' beloved dog. Hughes reveals that Spaz's real name is Duke and says that although he and the pooch developed a rapport, there is something to that adage about acting with children and animals, even if the actor is a child himself:

"Spaz was so cute and sweet, but one scene was hard to do with him. He just kept jumping up on me, trying to play, instead of walking beside me, so we had to do it over and over again."

Eleven year-old Hughes, unlike some of his older co-stars, was an avid *Spawn* reader and admits that he wanted the job "real bad." One of the movie's highlights for Hughes occurred when *Spawn* creator Todd McFarlane visited the set.

"He signed some comics for me and he bought all the cast and crew *Spawn* baseball caps and signed them too," Hughes recalls. "It was great to meet him."

A veteran of such special effects-laden films as *Wes Craven's New Nightmare* and *Pet Sematary*, Hughes enjoyed working with his animatronic co-star, the Violator: "It was fun working with the Violator. I have worked with mechanical puppets before, so they aren't scary to me. It was actually funny. When the effects men would make it move, it would sometimes wobble and look very awkward. So, when I had to act scared, I just imagined the scene was really happening."

Hughes has appeared in such films as *Apollo 13*, *Cops and Robbersons*, *Jack the Bear* and *Kindergarten Cop*. He has also provided voices for several animated television movies and appeared in telefilms like *Unspeakable Acts*, *Burden of Proof*, *The Jerry Sherwood Story* and *Dark Reflections*. Hughes has been a guest star on numerous television series, including *Picket Fences*, *Melrose Place*, *Beverly Hills 90210*, *Hangin' With Mr. Cooper* and *Doogie Howser*. 💀

CLOWN/ VIOLATOR

Clown is the 'human' form of the demon the Violator, cursed to appear as such for disobeying "the grand puppet master, Malebolgia, [who] creates Hellspawns to serve as commanders of his army for the inevitable final battle." Only the truly psychotic would dare to disregard Malebolgia's instructions. That would be Clown, played with demonic delight by John Leguizamo.

"Clown wants to usurp the power of Hell, basically. He wants to be The Man. He feels dissed when Malebolgia, the big devil, appoints Spawn instead," Leguizamo says. "So, even though he's assigned to sort of tutor Spawn, he wants to get him out of the way so he can lead the Army of Darkness. Obviously, the big boss thinks that he's too goofy. That's why he makes him Clown."

The film-makers turned to Leguizamo because they knew he could successfully balance Clown's demonic mean streak with his absurd sense of humour.

"He was just brilliant, because Clown is evil incarnate," Mark Dippé claims. "But what we wanted, and this is directly from the comic book, was a certain comedic element. Clown is sort of a screw-up from hell and a mean one. You don't want him mad at you, but he's also perversely funny. John brought

just that right mixture of humour and evil to the character."

Leguizamo was vaguely familiar with the *Spawn* comic book, but it was the lure of the *Spawn* toys that attracted him to the film version:

"I was in the middle of producing *The Pest* and these two guys come on the set with all these pictures and say, 'It would be wonderful to have you aboard.' I'm like, 'Yeah, whatever, OK, let me see.' Then they gave me a toy and I am easily sold on toys. So I started thinking about it and asking all my friends. Some of them were like, 'Yo man, *Spawn*, it's serious, that's the number one comic book.'"

Intrigued, Leguizamo began reading the book, to discover that his character was not exactly a superhero, but "... a five-foot tall, fat, 300 pound clown. I

started talking to Mark, to see how we might mould the character, make it maybe a little funnier and kookier."

This process continued throughout the shoot, as the ingenious Leguizamo came up with more gags and antics, inspired by the comic book: "The character was so full of life in the comic book. I read as many of the books as I could so I could lift the best lines out of them."

Leguizamo attributes the comic book's popularity to its unabashed dark humour, something he believes will set it apart from previous comic book-turned-films:

"Spawn goes for the jugular, has that aggressive thing that kids want and still has humour, character, story and the darkness you want in a superhero."

Clown's alter-ego, the Violator, certainly goes for the jugular. When the Violator first appears, Clown having transformed into "a massive, hulking beast with blood-red compound eyes and huge double-hinged, multi-fanged mandibles", Spawn is left impaled on a wall, soundly beaten.

The problems involved in creating this lethal, predatory and thirteen-foot tall "killing machine" could not be solved by model work alone. Director Mark Dippé explains: "Whenever you could see all the action and it lasted for five seconds, or when

there was a transformation — when Clown becomes the Violator, for instance — those would all have to be computer animation."

Of course, Spawn is not the first film in which Leguizamo's appearance has been altered. His role as the sensitive drag queen in To Wong Foo, Thanks for Everything, Julie Newmar required the actor to sport a fabulously gender-bending new look. His bravura performance earned him a Golden Globe nomination for Best Supporting Actor.

Subsequently, Leguizamo has starred in such films as William Shakespeare's Romeo & Juliet, as the hot-blooded, doomed Tybalt, Tony Scott's psychological thriller The Fan, and Executive Decision. Among his many other screen credits are Carlito's Way, Regarding Henry and Casualties of War.

Born in Bogota, Colombia, and raised in Manhattan, Leguizamo achieved critical acclaim for his off-Broadway one-man show, Mambo Mouth, which he wrote and performed.

On television, Leguizamo set a precedent by starring in the first Latin American comedy/variety show, House of Buggin, for the Fox network. He received an Emmy nomination and three Monitor Awards for his work on the series. Leguizamo first appeared on television as Calderone Jr on the popular series Miami Vice.

JASON WYNN

Martin Sheen plays the ruthless Jason Wynn, head of the secret agency that employed, among others, Al Simmons and Terry Fitzgerald. A formidable, Machiavellian figure, Wynn is obsessed with power and will sacrifice anything and anyone to obtain it. To that end, he orchestrates Al Simmons' death, part of a Faustian bargain he's made to achieve absolute, global hegemony. What he doesn't count on is Simmons' resurrection as Spawn.

"He basically wants to rule the world. Like every politician," Sheen says of Wynn. "He's an evil guy with no redeeming qualities, in league with the Devil."

Although Wynn is a comic book character, Sheen asserts that his nefarious, secret deeds are chillingly close to reality:

"So, making this guy the head of the CIA is not that far off. Jason is a classic 'spook', into dark intelligence operations and behaviour. But, he's taken it a step further and has his own personal agenda where he's running the world. Or at least he thinks he is."

Sheen was unfamiliar with the *Spawn* phenomenon when he was cast, but soon learned of the comic book's extraordinary appeal from a source close to home.

"I was sitting in the backyard and my oldest grandchild asked me what I'd be doing next, and I said, 'I'm going to do this film *Spawn*.' Well, he near-

ly fainted. He said, '*Spawn*? *Spawn*? The *Spawn*? It's only the most important comic book in the world.' He wanted to know all about it and he's the one who really cued me into how big the comic book was. I was just flabbergasted."

In keeping with his character's origins, Sheen painted Jason Wynn with "broad strokes."

"In film, we learn to be subtle, but this character's off a comic strip, so the overall approach was different, much bigger and more blatant." Sheen adds: "There's nothing subtle about this piece."

Sheen first attracted critical notice with his Broadway performance in *The Subject Was Roses*, which he recreated in the 1968 movie version. His portrayal of the indifferent killer in Terrence Malick's 1973 film *Badlands* won him further kudos. Sheen went on to star in Francis Ford Coppola's *Apocalypse Now*, as the military man assigned to assassinate the renegade officer played by Marlon Brando. Other films include *Catch-22*, *The Cassandra Crossing*, *Gandhi*, *That Championship Season*, *The Dead Zone*, *Firestarter*, *Wall Street* and *Da* (which he also executive produced). On television, he appeared as the convicted deserter in *The Execution of Private Slovik* and played John F. Kennedy in the mini-series *Kennedy*.

JESSICA PRIEST

Melinda Clarke portrays the beautiful, ambitious and evil assassin Jessica Priest. Employed by Jason Wynn, she is a sadistic killing machine, an exceptionally ruthless covert operative who uses her wits and sexuality to achieve incredibly lethal results. Ultra-ambitious, she sees her colleague Al Simmons as competition.

Clarke describes Priest as "... this type-A character, the number two operative in the agency. Simmons is number one and she doesn't like that. She is very ambitious and she is the classic vamp. She enjoys using her female powers to entice and get what she needs. She especially takes great pleasure in being the one that brings about the demise of Al Simmons."

Although Priest is quite familiar with all sorts of exotic weapons and an exceptionally capable killer, Clarke is not a gun *aficionado* and had to train in order to feel comfortable with them:

"I don't really like guns, I don't see the appeal of them. I had to train with a weapons expert and learned that I could enjoy myself as long as I respected the weapon."

Raised in Dana Point, California, Clarke participated in workshops with the prestigious South Coast Repertory, before honing her acting abilities at the Idyllwilde School of Music and Arts.

No stranger to science fiction films, Clarke has appeared in such genre movies as *Killer Tongue*, for which she won the Best Actress Award at the 1996 Sitges Fantasy Film Festival, and *Return of the Living Dead III*. Her other film credits include *Critics* and *Return to Two-Moon Junction*.

On television Clarke stars as the exotic and mysterious Margo Vincent in the action series *Soldier of Fortune*. As well as having appeared in *Nash Bridges*, *Xena: Warrior Princess*, *Sliders* and *Seinfeld*, among others, she was a series regular on the daytime drama *Days of Our Lives*, in which she starred with her father, actor John Clarke.

MALEBOLGIA

The *Spawn Bible*, the official guide to the many and varied characters that inhabit Spawn's comic-strip world, describes Malebolgia as "more cunning than all those previous [demons]. More vicious. More cruel."

The supreme master of Hell, this *über*-demon's greatest strength is the Army of Darkness he has created, a force that one day will attack Heaven itself. These Hellspawns are both his soldiers and his greatest entertainment. A diabolical puppet-master, Malebolgia offers bargains and false promises, before cruelly heaping torment upon torment. He enjoys nothing more than to play with the souls of those he corrupts.

None, though, have provided Malebolgia more gleefully sadistic joy than Al Simmons. For unlike the many before him, he sold his soul for a pittance, the fragile human emotion we call love. How he enjoyed seeing Simmons' pain when he realised what he had become, and that the woman he cherished above all else was lost to him forever.

With the advent of the deadly nerve gas Heat 16 comes the final twist of the knife, the vengeful act that will both bind Simmons to Malebolgia forever and unleash the armies of Hell on Earth...

Like the Violator, Malebolgia was brought to life in the movie through a combination of model work and digital magic. The effects wizards at KNB EFX laboured long and hard to push back the boundaries of what had previously been seen on screen by creating a totally virtual Hell, complete with an army of hungry souls.

And they did a *damned* fine job. ☠

ong Kong airport: a black-clad assassin, armed with an AK-830 missile launcher, impassively targets and obliterates a plane and its occupants. He is Al Simmons, a covert operative for an intra-governmental organisation known only as A-6. No emo-tion shows on his face. He's done this before. Many times.

Watching the devastation unfold is an old man, Cogliostro, his hard and coldly mystical eyes registering dismay but no surprise.

Simmons retreats to the warmth of his house in the suburbs, seeking comfort in the arms of his fiancée Wanda Blake. But when he discovers twenty-six innocent civilians died as a result of his actions, Simmons resolves to quit the business entirely.

However, Simmons' boss Jason Wynn has other plans. In exchange for his engineering a profoundly powerful biological weapon known as Heat 16, the vile and perverse Clown and his demonic master Malebolgia have promised Wynn world domination. And part of the bargain is Wynn's top operative, Al Simmons.

As Simmons confronts Wynn in his office at the A-6 complex, the sensual and deadly Jessica Priest, another agency operative and Simmons' competitor, mocks her co-worker's would-be pacifism. But

Above: *Hong Kong airport. Simmons' targets de-plane, unaware they are seconds from death.*

Right: *An icy confrontation between A-6 operatives Jessica Priest (Melinda Clarke) and Al Simmons (Michael Jai White).*

open.

Not only have five years passed, but Simmons has become a huge, horribly charred and disfigured creature. Wracked with pain, he meets Clown, who is both welcoming and deriding, further adding to Simmons' confusion. Disoriented, he staggers through a city of filth, violence and poverty, rebuffing offers of help from a young boy, Zack Webb, and Cogliostro.

Simmons returns to his house and discovers

Simmons is adamant. "If you want someone filling bodybags, send Priest," he tells Wynn. Disingenuously, Wynn accepts his resignation, but only if Simmons agrees to one last mission. A North Korean refinery producing biochemical weapons requires neutralisation.

Simmons agrees, but on reaching the refinery's core is greeted by Wynn himself, who informs him that "priorities have changed." Wynn's goal is now to detonate the killer chemicals, testing them on the inhabitants of a nearby town. Horrified, Simmons tries to stop him, only to be gunned down by Priest, who then engages a nozzle on her gun and sprays a clear, highly flammable gelatine all over Simmons' face and body. Wynn flicks a cigarette, and Simmons ignites in a sickening silhouette of flame.

Simmons' burnt corpse plummets to Hell. Through curtains of magma-flame, the massive, hulking, godless creature that is Malebolgia offers peals of laughter. Simmons struggles in pain and torment, an image of Wanda's face glimpsed through the flames. Just as she screams, Simmons' eyes snap

Right: *Spawn's living suit begins to emerge, as the gleeful Clown (John Leguizamo) looks on.*

Below left and right: *Spawn crashes the Swiss Embassy party.*

Wanda still lives there, but now with her new family. She has married Simmons' best friend and fellow A-6 operative Terry Fitzgerald, and together they have a young daughter, Cyan. Overcome, Simmons collapses, and is discovered by his faithful terrier, Spaz, and Cyan, who approaches Simmons, unafraid. Wanda and Terry, fearing the repulsive stranger, threaten to call the police.

Clown, on the scene as a party entertainer, intercedes, leading Simmons away to a graveyard. There, Simmons sees his own grave and realises the terrible truth. He has literally died and gone to Hell. Clown explains that Simmons is now Spawn, the designated leader of Hell's legion. It was his love for Wanda and his despair at losing her that made him agree to join the ranks of the Devil.

Suddenly convulsed with pain, Simmons' body transforms, growing a hard exterior armour known as necroplasm that responds to his thoughts and emotions, manifesting special, innate defences. Some punks, performing a black mass at the graveyard, get more than they bargained for as they witness the shocking emergence of Spawn's living suit.

At a party in the Swiss Embassy, Fitzgerald and Wynn are startled when the ballroom's stained-glass dome explodes and Spawn sails down, his giant cape trailing behind him. First grabbing Wynn by the throat, Spawn sends him crashing across the room. Spawn is only prevented from doing further damage by the arrival of Priest, who peppers his body with bullets. Miraculously, his wounds heal in front of his eyes and protective armour rises over his face.

Left: *The fall of Priest. Clown applauds Spawn's 'murderous propensity'.*

Below: *Jason Wynn undergoes surgery to have an implant connected to his heartbeat.*

The two commence battle, Spawn eventually pinning his adversary against a high balcony railing. Ever defiant, Priest taunts him. "You don't have the guts," she says, but a moment later Priest crashes through the railing, tumbling to the floor. The ubiquitous Clown, dressed as a waiter, applauds Spawn's murderous propensity as gun-toting A-6 agents fill the room. Shot repeatedly, Spawn is blown backwards through a window, but his chains instinctively sprout, grasping the Embassy's outer wall and breaking his fall. As the guards open fire again, Spawn's cape turns into a huge, ribbed wing, and, stunned, he soars away into the night.

Afterwards, Wynn quarrels with Clown, but they finally agree that Wynn will have an implant inserted, connecting his heartbeat to the Heat 16 missiles. "That way, no smartass would dare take you out," Clown reasons.

The next day, Spawn follows Wanda to school, where he plays with Cyan and Spaz, the latter elect-

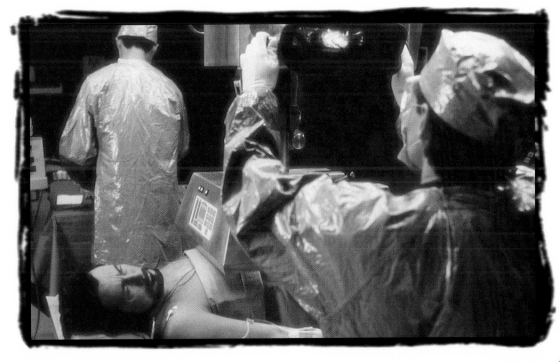

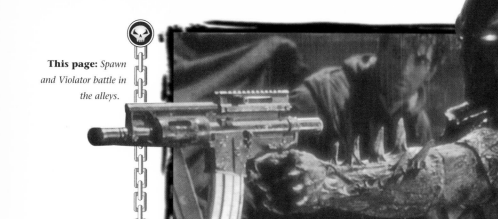

This page: *Spawn and Violator battle in the alleys.*

ing to stay with him as he proceeds to his new home, a crumbling alley. There, Spawn once more encounters Zack and the two begin to form a friendly rapport.

Clown reveals Wynn is just a small pawn in a larger, more malevolent scheme involving Heat 16, and that he, Spawn, is destined to become the destroyer of worlds. Staggered, Spawn reneges on the promise he made in Hell, and Clown seizes on the opportunity to teach him a lesson. He transforms into the Violator, and the two lock horns, the conflict spilling into the alley.

The Violator is impaled on an electrical hydrant, but fights back — using Zack to turn the battle and leaving Spawn pinned on the spikes of a wrought iron fence.

Cogliostro appears, revealing that he is an immortal, like Spawn, a 500 year-old warrior and assassin who has devoted himself to the destruction of the Devil and his legion. He now believes that he has found his successor in Spawn.

Under Cogliostro's tutelage, Spawn practices manipulating his living suit, and in short order these new abilities are put to the test. Riding a 'bor-

rowed' motorcycle, and chased by Clown on an immense, hazardous waste truck, Spawn wills his cape to form an impervious barrier and then anchors his armour into the asphalt. The truck hits this new obstacle at high speed and explodes.

Terry Fitzgerald, meanwhile, has compiled a disk detailing Wynn's nefarious schemes and is in the process of leaking it to the media when Wynn himself arrives at his house. Holding Wanda and Cyan at gunpoint, Wynn blasts Terry's computer to bits.

Spawn arrives at the house to discover Hell has poured forth from what was once the fireplace. In the centre of this infernal setting is a terrified Wanda, bound to an arcane rack and terrorised by Wynn, who holds a serrated blade to her neck. Either Spawn joins them in their demonic scheme or Wanda dies.

To Spawn's horror, Wynn takes his silence literally and plunges the blade into Wanda. Overcome with fury, Spawn makes to throw Wynn into the fiery portal, despite the knowledge that his death will unleash the Heat 16 missiles. The fires in the portal blaze, growing more violent and compelling. He is about to send Wynn into them, but hesitates. "I'm through doing Hell's dirty work," he says.

Instead, Spawn returns to Wanda's lifeless body, which kicks Spawn away with surprising strength. With the knife still buried in her chest, Wanda climbs off the rack and admonishes Spawn for not avenging her death. Frozen in shock, Spawn stares, allowing Clown, who has shape-shifted to appear as Wanda, to wound him. As he exhorts Spawn to kill Wynn, the hordes of Hell wait, ready to cross over... ☻

Left: *Spawn's cape becomes an impervious shield during the motorbike chase.*

Below left: *Wynn prepares to 'kill' Wanda (Theresa Randle).*

Below right: *Will he, won't he? Spawn considers Wynn's future, or lack thereof.*

SPAWN
BEHIND THE SCENES

PRODUCTION DESIGN

Much of the *Spawn* comic's incredible success can be accredited to Todd McFarlane's moody and evocative artwork, and particularly his meticulously observed contrasts between the darkly Gothic alleys and churches which form Spawn's home territory, and the ultra-modern, sterile environs in which the criminal and government élite ply their trade. Add to this the warm, idyllic home which Wanda Blake shares with husband Terry Fitzgerald and their daughter Cyan, a setting in direct juxtapostion to Spawn's anguished existence, and you have a rich brew of varying locales and moods to bring to life on the screen.

Director Mark Dippé and his crew met the chal-

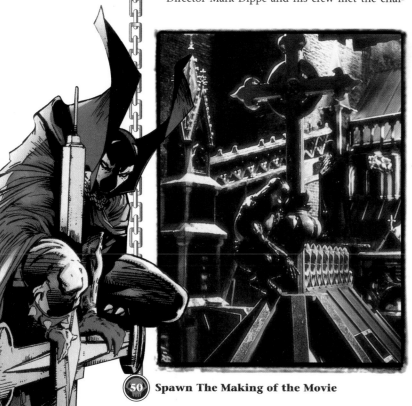

lenge head on, and rather than discarding the comic's already established backdrops, as with some other comic-to-film adaptations, embraced them. The film's look, Dippé explains, echoed the shadowy palette of the comic book:

"I like the macabre, Dante-esque aspects of the *Spawn* story, as well as Todd's amazing visual illustrations. I wanted the atmosphere to be dark and mysterious, a no-man's land, someplace between Heaven and Hell. Not a totally evil place, where everyone is a junkie or a murderer, but where a few good people are cast away for a variety of reasons.

"When I began to work on the script, the thing that struck me was this throughline in the comic: life is cruel and the good guys don't always win. It's similar to stories in the Bible or classic Greek myths.

The world isn't simple. These guys from Hell are nasty, but the good guys, like angry gods, could strike you down too. I wanted the look of the film to reflect all that."

Production designer Philip Harrison, whose various film credits range from Peter Hyams' horror/suspense film *The Relic* to Alan Parker's historical drama *Mississippi Burning*, created this murky world. Interpreting such a popular comic book for the screen

was a formidable task, even for this veteran artist.

"Designing a movie is always a challenge, but *Spawn* was even more so, as I had to put a very successful comic book with a very devoted following into three-dimensional form," Harrison comments.

As in the comic book, Harrison relied on a dark palette, but tailored the sets to the charcters. For instance, the evil Jason Wynn's forbidding, high-tech office was sleek and severe, its hard, blatant

This page and opposite: *Philip Harrison's epic rooftop cathedral sets, and the production designs that spawned them.*

Right: Detail from the cathedral set's Gothic architecture.

Below: Spawn's alley, as originally envisaged.

Opposite: The North Korean refinery as concept and from the movie.

angles accented in glossy black and chrome. Spawn's environment was more obscure, a nihilistic, Gothic place, full of shadows and fear. A futuristic nightmare, it featured a Byzantine bunker of crumbling alleys and decaying buildings, overlooked by the "... expansive roof of a former Gothic cathedral turned street mission... rundown and long neglected, the cathedral is in the advanced stages of disrepair." What appeared on screen as one decrepit city was, in fact, various sets, locations and digital alche-

my, the latter designed to broaden the landscape.

"Spawn's church rooftop and alley set were conceived as a contiguous whole," explains Harrison, "but in fact they were a combination of several set pieces, locations and an optical composite planned to give a very wide establishing shot or shots. The rooftop set itself filled a large stage almost completely and I gave it a grimy, smoke-blackened and rotted stone finish. The alley, several stories below this, had some recognisable elements of the rooftop

Right and far right: *The alley in which Spawn takes refuge was designed with recognisable elements from the rooftop sets.*

Below: *The alley as it appeared in the comic.*

architecture in order to tie the two sets together in the audience's mind."

This ominous rooftop vista reappeared on stage in the form of a giant trans-light, a photo backing of the set lit from behind by movie lights.

"We created the rooftop of an abandoned Gothic cathedral with a 150 degree trans-lit view of the set, so you could see the city and a three-tiered alley set built to the grids of the soundstage," executive producer Alan Blomquist explains.

The alley, where Spawn finds a kind of solace, was a combination of soundstage and location work. The production filmed the latter on a downtown street in LA, populating it with garish and brutal denizens, as played by enthusiastic extras. Harrison's department created the alley's sinister nooks and crannies, filled with the urban detritus of the disenfranchised.

"Within the alley, there was an elaborate homeless warren of hovels made from junk and industrial discard, which matched the downtown LA location. All of this put Spawn firmly into a world which exists, although it is perhaps a heightened reality," Harrison says.

The production used another existing location to double as the Swiss Embassy, in which a party becomes anything but neutral. At this event Spawn wreaks his revenge on Jason Wynn and reveals his new prowess, things that Harrison had to keep in mind when designing the set. In fact, as Harrison recalls, he had to create a set that would be demolished:

"The rotunda from the LA Museum of Natural History became the setting for Spawn's first public appearance, so to speak, at a reception where he displays some of his spectacular powers. I needed to provide some break-away elements, in this case large mirrors, flower displays, lamps and, of course, food."

Harrison also designed a comfortable living room, Spawn's home in a former life. Its centrepiece, a once-inviting hearth, became an ominous fireplace, serving as the Devil's portal. Indeed, the mantel and the room itself, under demonic sway, would come to life through computer magic, but Harrison had to create surroundings that were so incredibly, reliably ordinary that this hellish transformation would seem even more horrific.

"The living room and Hell's portal in Spawn's for-

Far left: *The interior set for the Swiss Embassy scenes.*

Left: *Martin Sheen and some 'break-away' elements.*

Below: *Wanda and Terry's home, with enough room to swing a Violator.*

mer home," Harrison explains, "gave me an opportunity to contrast between previously established domestic normalcy and the nightmare subjectivity of the Hell portal. This was a good example of how, with the digitising processes now available to the film-maker, the designer's technical burden has been lightened, freeing the imagination as never before."

All these soundstage interiors had to accommo-date the usual cadre of crew members and the standard film equipment, consisting of cameras, camera mounts, the occasional crane, dolly tracks, lights, screens, flags and c-stands. However, Harrison also had to build sets that were tall and wide enough to harbour a ten-foot hydraulic puppet, the horrible creature known as the Violator, a technological masterpiece with an array of facial articulation, gesturing arms and a gyrating body. 💀

COSTUMES

A creature born again from the depths of Hell wearing a living, emotive suit of arcane necro-flesh; a demonic, clown-suited, five foot nothing bundle of twisted attitude; the shadowy, power-dressed head of a covert intra-governmental agency; a lethal yet highly desirable assassin swathed in body-formed black leather. The wealth and variety of visual imagery in *Spawn* extended not just to the production designers, but to the man who was responsible for visualising and dressing the cast members, costume designer Dan Lester.

Spawn marks Lester's fourth movie with production designer Philip Harrison and the two enjoyed a happy collaboration.

"I had just done *The Relic* with Philip," recalls Lester, "and that had some creatures in it, so I had some experience with this sort of stuff. We've both worked with [director] Peter Hyams a lot and he shoots stuff dark, so I had a pretty good idea of what kind of colours work. I had done a lot of action

movies, I'd done a big party scene, I've dealt with a lot of the elements in *Spawn* before."

As part of his research, Lester combed through several issues of the comic book and derived his colour scheme from them:

"This is an adult comic book and it is characterised by dark, deep tones. When I first did the palette, everything was in dark tones. The only place in the whole movie where we saw pastels, soft colours and whites, was the birthday party for Wanda's daughter, Cyan."

At the Embassy party, Lester also added richer colours to the women's wardrobes, their bright, beguiling evening gowns highlighting his sombre canvas. Lester describes the scene: "The men were mostly dressed in black, but the women wore jewel tones, golds and reds."

Wanda, Spawn's true love, also wore more saturated colours, to underscore her integrity and spirit.

"We tried to keep Wanda in golds and burgundies and purples, again jewel tones, as well as earth-

Right: *The Swiss Embassy party gave Dan Lester the chance to add richer colours to the film's generally more sombre tones.*

related colours, to emphasise her down-to-earth nature," says Lester.

Angela, Spawn's angelic nemesis from the comic, makes a subtle cameo appearance at the Embassy party, though not in her usual attire of a barely dressed swirl of warrior 'ribbons'. In fact, blink and you'll miss her as she brushes past Jason Wynn. Wearing a figure-hugging gown and cape ensemble, the sole clue to her identity is her Spawn earrings, glimpsed only momentarily.

Because Spawn's suit was a prosthetic piece and a computer derived image, Lester really only dressed his alter-ego Al Simmons. His nefarious career in covert operations dictated his wardrobe, as it did for his boss Jason Wynn.

"Simmons was a secret agent and everything in the agency was dark blues and greys, so [he] starts out wearing the same colours," comments Lester. "Wynn pretty much looked the way he did in the comics, those dark power suits. We broadened the shoulders a little bit, to make him appear more over-the-top, but we tried to match the comic."

For Lester, "the star of the movie is Clown", as played by John Leguizamo. Initially, director Mark Dippé instructed Lester to remain true to the comic book's essence without actually replicating it. However, after several sketches and much debate, both agreed that the best look was that closest to the comic book designs. Lester explains:

"We ended up screen-testing a version of what is in the comic, but making subtle changes. We had to get all the fabrics to reflect the comic book colours but, as Mark put it, 'We want this guy to look like [he] just pulled his clothes out of a dumpster.' So, the stuff is really filthy."

The grimy clothes, in an array of fabrics and textures, retained their underlying garish hues, not only because they hearkened back to the comic book but also because the shadowy, spooky film lighting demanded bright colours.

"They all started with these really bright, acidy colours," says Lester. "His pants were fluorescent purple stripes, the top was a green and black velour, 'puke green', like a little kid's shirt. We hand-painted flames on the sleeves and back of his leather jacket, to represent Hell, and then we really, really aged it a great deal, so it looked filthy. As it turned out, we shot [the scene] so dark that we needed the colours that were buried there."

Although this was Clown's primary outfit, his

mischief occasionally demanded a more appropriate wardrobe.

"They added a few bits where he shows up as a cheerleader," says Lester. "It was hysterical and John, who is so creative and original, really played it well."

Lester adds that despite this dramatic change of attire, they remained true to what they'd already established in terms of colour for the character:

"Essentially, his cheerleading outfit was the colour of vomit too, and that was the idea. He's supposed to be disgusting and so the clothes were all day-glo greens, citrus yellows and avocados; colours you wouldn't want to put together on purpose. It worked out great."

Though Lester lavished considerable thought on Clown's look, he was no less attentive to the supporting cast.

Melinda Clarke played the beautiful, lethal and thoroughly evil Jessica Priest, one of Wynn's dedicated operatives. Although she was as reprehensible and brutal as Clown, Priest's wardrobe, by contrast, reflected her blatant sexuality and confidence.

"Because she worked at the agency," details Lester, "she started out in these blues and greys, but wardrobe always played up her feral sexuality. When we first see her in Wynn's office, we see a little gun peeking out of her skirt. She eventually got into this very severe, stylised, second-skin leather suit. She was a very sexy babe."

As for Cogliostro, "... he was supposed to be a very mythic character. In the comic books, he always wears this long overcoat. We kept him in a long cloak for part of the movie, but I talked to Mark and I said, 'Why don't we have his clothes help reflect where he comes from, since he is a 500 or 600 year-old soldier?' By the end of the film, he is in a studded tunic and chain mail from the Middle Ages, in tones of brown and gold."

Above: *Melinda Clarke as Jessica Priest. Lethal in leather.*

Right: *For the alley scenes, the costumes went 'Gothic'.*

Opposite: *Pre-production Priest.*

Clown's jacket and Priest's cat-suit:

"Leather works really well. You can get the shine from it, but it's got flexibility and it moulds to the body. You can oil it up to get a sheen that kicks off the lights, even in low lighting."

Though Spawn's arcane look was designed and implemented by the make-up and special creature effects specialists at KNB EFX, and enhanced in terms of its otherworldly tendencies by the computer effects wizards at ILM, as far as actor Michael Jai White was concerned, it still amounted to a costume he had to wear each day and then endure hours of intense action under glaring studio lights.

The actor had to don phosphorescent yellow contact lenses and a fitted, rubbery body suit, its exterior a sculptural combination of muscles, sinews and charred flesh, the result of Al Simmons' transformation to Spawn. The contacts irritated the actor's eyes and the suit subjected his body to sweltering temperatures that left him "... sweating constantly. Once the suit went on, I was like a crock pot. I was marinating in my own juices," White remembers. "I was under a great deal of physical duress, in terms of that costume. I started sweating the minute I put on the head piece and the suit. It was hot and itching and burning and those sensations might cause you to drift. I used that as a mental exercise, concentrating straight through to my objective, and each time that strengthened my will. I had to preserve my energy, both mentally and physically, until we shot and then I had to focus on the scene."

Though designed to send a shiver down the spine of both adversary and cinema-goer alike, White's

Above: Priest dresses to kill.

Right: The Spawn suit from the comic.

Far right: One of the punks from the graveyard scene.

Lester also had to garb the extras populating the future that Spawn rejoins five years after Al Simmons' death. The extras, Lester points out, helped him establish the feel of this new 'netherworld':

"We tried to use existing clothes for the background players, but we made pieces in comic book colours, to try to bring up the light a little. A lot of golds, rich blues. In the script, everything goes a little more Gothic. There are only 'Haves' and 'Have-Nots'. The middle class has disappeared and it's a much, much nastier world."

Lester found that the best material for such a dark and horrid place was leather, which he used on both

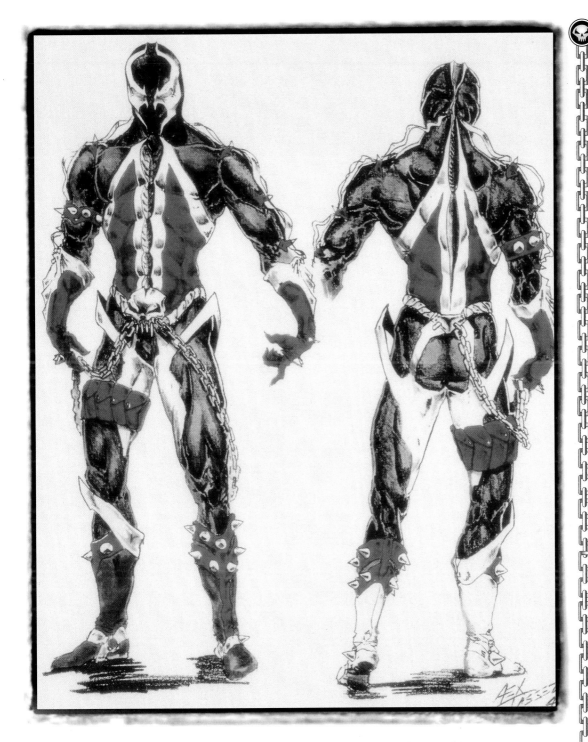

Spawn suit also managed to unnerve fellow cast member Theresa Randle:

"When I saw Michael in his Spawn suit, it was not that difficult to act frightened because I scare easily and it was pretty awful looking. Sydney [Beaudoin (Cyan)], I think, maybe had one encounter with him where she was afraid, but after that she was fine. Her innocence as a little girl really came across with this Spawn character because she was so pure and naïve, and it's easier for children to make believe."

MAKE-UP

efore they could become Spawn and Clown, actors Michael Jai White and John Leguizamo had to brave hours of painstakingly applied prosthetics, as administered under the auspices of the artists in charge of special make-up and creature effects: Robert Kurtzman, Greg Nicotero and Howard Berger, collectively known as KNB EFX.

Formed in 1988, KNB EFX's work has graced such films as *Mars Attacks!*, creating duplicates of Glenn Close, Pierce Brosnan and Sarah Jessica Parker; *Eraser*, for which they invented hydraulic alligators; *Jingle All the Way*, designing Arnold Schwarzenegger's 'Turboman' suit; and the sci-fi comedy *Men in Black*, on which they collaborated with famed effects wizard Rick Baker to provide several aliens. Other film credits include Quentin Tarantino's *Pulp Fiction*, *From Dusk Till Dawn*, *Jungle 2 Jungle*, *Misery* and *Casino*. The company has also worked on such television shows as *The X Files* and

The Outer Limits.

The exhaustive process of building prosthetic second skins required both White and Leguizamo to sit motionless and silent as sculpted latex pieces were dusted, lacquered, painted and glued to their faces, heads and necks. The 'silent' and 'motionless' part was particularly difficult for the gregarious, loquacious Leguizamo, whose transformation into Clown

Above right: *Greg Nicotero at KNB EFX.*

Below right: *John Leguizamo begins the 'exhaustive' prosthetic application process.*

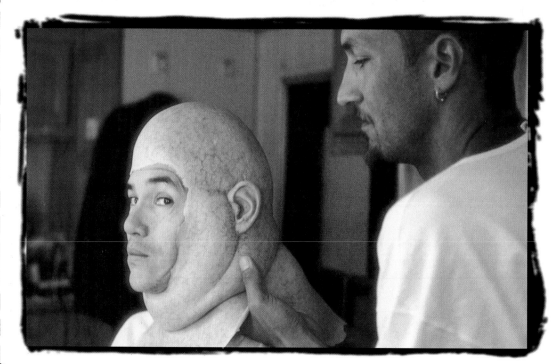

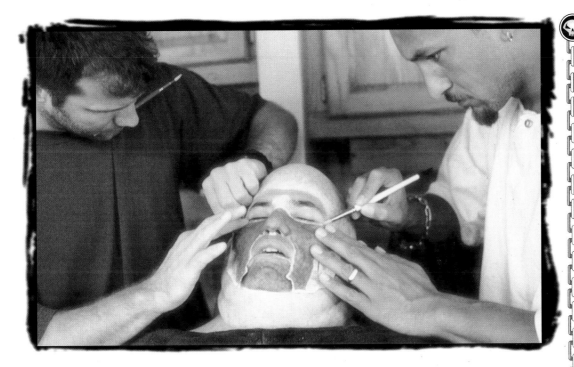

**Left and centre
left:** *Latex cowl,
acrylic paint and pro-
said adhesive complete
the transformation.*

Below: *A pre-
production character
study of Clown.*

uizamo says. "It was just incredible, exactly what I'd pictured from the comic book. They just transformed me into this mean, short, fat clown, with an evil blue face that captured the sinister humour that character has. It was the closest transition from page to screen that I've ever seen."

One of the greatest challenges for Leguizamo, beyond the uncomfortable suit and prosthetic devices, was Clown's height, a foot shorter than Leguizamo.

"John is an extremely talented, versatile actor,

included a latex cowl affixed to his slicked-back hair, a thick coat of acrylic paint and prosaid adhesive painted on his face, which was thereupon airbrushed and outlined in black, indelible ink. Finally, a twenty-pound fat suit with foam latex hands, which effectively obscured what remained of the agile actor's form, was added to complete the transformation.

"We were a little sceptical initially," Howard Berger recalls. "We had to build so much rubber, we knew it would be tough on John. This kind of thing can be very scary because it is so confining and inhibits movement drastically. But, we didn't realise who we were dealing with. John had so much enthusiasm, he made the whole character infinitely better and more entertaining than we could have imagined. He was such a great performer and really exciting to watch. He didn't let the suit intimidate him."

Leguizamo's admiration for KNB helped overcome any initial fears.

"I was just amazed by the prosthetic work," Leg-

both comedic and dramatic, but Clown was supposed to be 4'6" and John is 5'8"," director Mark Dippé recalls. "I said, 'John, you have to squat or we'll tie your legs to your knees or something', and he says, 'No, man, I can't do it, my knees are soft.' Finally, after cajoling him, he agreed, and essentially he squatted on his haunches to be 4'6" the whole time. He had to walk, talk, dance and act like this. He'd do a take, sweating like a madman, although we couldn't see it because it was inside [of his prosthetics] and when I'd call 'cut,' he'd just fall down, he'd give up and crash to the floor. It was extremely physically demanding."

Leguizamo explains that "... Mark was so relaxed and just had so much confidence that I easily trusted him. I think the stress [of making a movie] gave him a sort of Zen-like quality, especially when I came up with different ideas for Clown. At first he'd say, 'We can't add all those things. It's not gonna work.' Then, he'd relax into this really Zen, Buddha-like thing. 'Okay, John, whatever you say, let's try it.' I had a great time, even if it was sometimes painful."

Leguizamo's fellow artist Michael Jai White also suffered through twelve to fourteen hours a day encased inside a rubber suit and mask. The character, disfigured through a fiery death and hellish rebirth/transformation, required elaborate and exhaustive make-up. While the comic book delineated Spawn's overall appearance, the experts at KNB EFX had to alter it slightly for the film.

"We were dealing with a known quantity, but the most difficult part was modifying the character,"

Above: *The 5'8" tall Leguizamo had to squat throughout filming to become the 4'6" Clown.*

Right: *One of several designs for Spawn's disfigured appearance.*

Opposite: *KNB EFX's make-up experts begin work on Spawn's rubber head.*

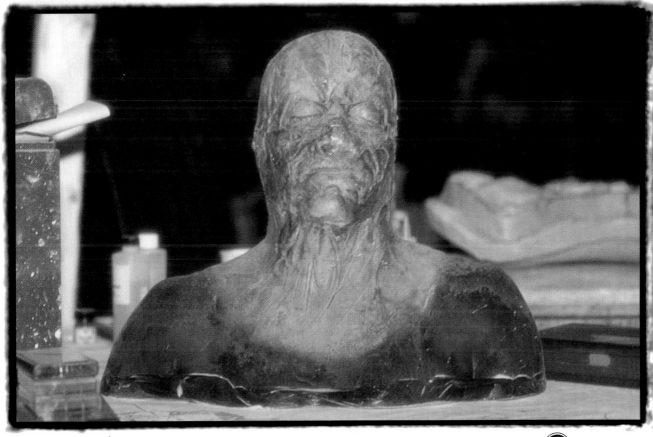

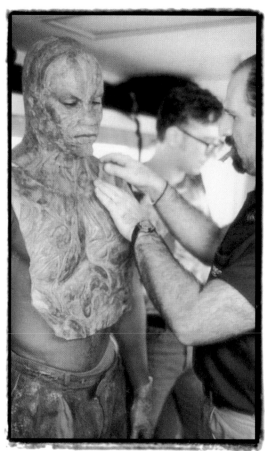

explains Greg Nicotero. "For instance, in the comic book, he has no nose. We had to deal with how to hide the actor's nose as much as possible, because the film-makers wanted to simulate that it had been burned off in Al Simmons' death."

The arduous process began months before cameras rolled, a period of "research and development" in which KNB EFX worked with White to create the most effective rendition of Spawn that would also be personalised to the actor playing him.

"We got Michael in, took a head cast, and sculpted different versions of him," Nicotero remembers. "We made several busts and laid all the prosthetics down on one of Michael's heads and tried four different paint jobs."

KNB EFX, in consultation with the film-makers, selected a favourite head and tested its look on film. That camera test not only required Michael to don the phoney head, "... glued on to him like an extra layer of skin", but also dentures and contact lenses. Nicotero continues:

"We tried the full gamut of devices because you can't really determine that final look until you see how it will read on film. We dealt with synthetic material, like latex, which absorbs light differently than our skin. If you see it with the naked eye, it will look one way and it may seem completely different on film. Not to mention the fact that once they start

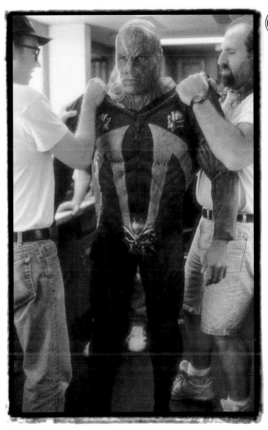

lighting it, that changes it too. So, we needed to see what colours photographed, how they photographed, and how the lighting responded to them. It also gave Michael the opportunity to practice wearing a rubber head."

Spawn's mask was not just one piece but many separate ones, each glued to his head, neck, chin, nose, cheeks and forehead, which was one of the reasons the application process took so long. Nicotero points out that "... the reason we do prosthetics in individual pieces is to allow the actor more flexibility, in terms of his expressions. If it was all one piece, once it was glued around the lips and eyes, it really wouldn't allow much of an expressive range. Whereas this approach enabled Michael to emote."

Although the hot, uncomfortable make-up and requisite prosthetic parts provided White with an actual feel for Spawn's constant physical pain, it was White's ability to convey Spawn's despair and conflict, producer Clint Goldman muses, that gave the character life:

"Michael's task, in terms of portraying Spawn, was extremely challenging in that he's the title character and everybody already has an image of Spawn from the comic books. He had to find a way to make the character live on screen, to act almost in spite of the suit, after enduring hours of make-up and preparation every day."

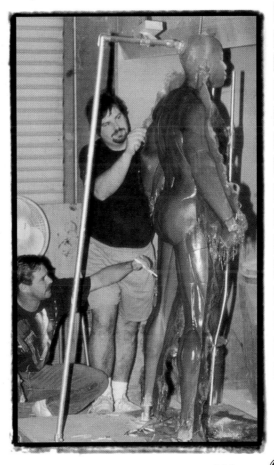

Opposite above: *KNB EFX's amazing creature workshop.*

Opposite below: *The puppet of Malebolgia takes shape.*

Left: *The thirteen-foot hydraulic Violator.*

Below: *An 'insert' leg for the Violator.*

Of course, Spawn's diabolical enemy, the Violator, only existed as puppets or as computer-created images. KNB EFX designed and created the former, based on the comic book illustrations and on the type of action Dippé required of them.

"We had a thirteen-foot hydraulic Violator, with full facial and arm articulation and a moving torso with the ability to pivot at the waist," Nicotero says. "We also used a lab puppet which was basically an oversized marionette, also about thirteen-feet tall, which was manipulated by puppeteers using rods and wires. For most of the close-up work, we used an insert head, which was a bust of the Violator with arms ending at the elbows, articulating mandible horns that shot out of the side of the head and a horn on the top that moved in a telescoping, striking way. We also had several insert hands that were also articulated and insert legs for a variety of different shots."

Much of the second-unit film work, which often involved just the puppets, was directed by Steve Williams. This distribution of duties proved efficacious, since Williams, as animation director, also knew how much of the Violator could effectively work as a computer image. Thus, he knew exactly what to glean from the puppets' "live-action performances" in order to combine them with their computer-animated counterparts. 💀

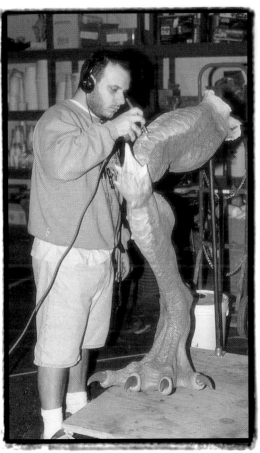

FILMING

rom the initial meeting between Clint Goldman, Mark Dippé and New Line and the start of principal photography, about four years elapsed. During this period, Dippé and Alan McElroy honed the script while Goldman, Dippé and Steve "Spaz" Williams outlined the visual effects. Then Goldman and Dippé started work with casting director Mary Jo Slater, as well as scouting locations and conferring with the artists who would eventually comprise the behind-the-scenes team, including cinematographer Guillermo Navarro, production designer Philip Harrison, costume designer Dan Lester and the special make-up and creature effects team KNB EFX, personified by Robert Kurtzman, Greg Nicotero and Howard Berger.

The film shot on various locations around Los Angeles, including Pasedena, Pacific Palisades and the downtown area, before moving to Raleigh Studios and Hollywood Center Studios for sound stage work. As second unit director/animation director, Williams split his time between the LA production and his former employer ILM in northern California, where some of the film's many visual effects were accomplished.

Above right: *Director Mark Dippé (left) and producer Clint Goldman confer on the set of* Spawn.

Below right: *Just a few of the many hundreds of storyboard sequences utilised and 'evolved' by the filmmakers in the course of the shoot.*

The film-makers also established elaborate story-boards, which served as visual guides to each scene. However, Dippé points out that the storyboards were not gospel:

"You have to be flexible, because once you get out on set and really start to do the work everything is not always exactly as planned. A movie is an evolving being. It's not as if you can control it just by saying, 'You will be exactly this.' Unless you have a ton of money there is always some unforeseen constraint where you find yourself saying, 'I've got an hour and I've got to do this and I can't get the camera high enough.' So you change it."

The mutability of the production process became evident early in the picture. Only a few weeks into principal photography, Dippé decided to revamp a pivotal sequence, taking it from live-action to the computer. After designing a model for Hell, which manifests itself at the film's end, and running elaborate tests, creating intricate 'concept' drawings and generally proceeding along one course, the film-makers decided to attempt the sequence digitally.

Of the various sets used during primary filming, one of the most spectacular, the cathedral rooftop, was constructed at the Hollywood Center. Though, ultimately, these practical sets would be but a portion of the movie's landscape. The vista was broadened in post-production with virtual models and virtual sets. The church roof did, however, become the launching pad for a stunt between Violator and Spawn. In this sequence, Violator pins Spawn to the railing, Spawn fires his gun, and both fall to the alley below. The stunt, as originally conceived, only required the Spawn stunt double to tumble to the cushions below. The brittle Violator rod puppet, attached to a cable, was to remain safely suspended.

"What we had intended to do," explains visual effects producer Tom Peitzman, "was just release the slack in the cable so it looked like Violator fell, but

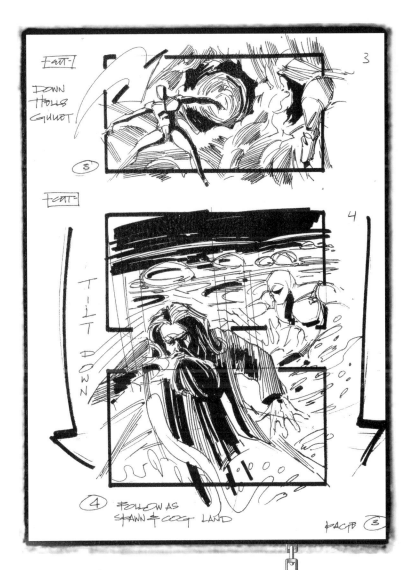

what happened was when the stuntman went over, so did the puppet, and it landed on top of him. It was hilarious actually, and the shot's in the movie."

The various animatronic incarnations of Violator proved very popular with the crew members' children, who often visited the set. The neighbourhood kids, however, were more interested in John Leguizamo in his Clown regalia. Several loitered around his trailer, enticed and terrified by the strange thing he'd become. The good-natured Leguizamo often obliged them by serving up his own brand of shocking terror, causing the giggling children to scamper to safety.

Stunts factored heavily into *Spawn*, as many of the comic book characters possessed super-human strength and skills. Additionally, Spawn, avenging angel and pugnacious pugilist, used his powers in several fight and flight sequences. The choreography of such scenes fell to stunt coordinator Charles Croughwell.

One of the first and most spectacular scenes

Above: *From the original storyboards, Spawn and Cogliostro descend to Hell.*

Left: *The Violator puppet, pre-downfall.*

Right: John
Leguizamo clowns
around.

Below: Michael Jai
White's stunt double
prepares to drop in on
the Swiss Embassy
party.

Opposite: From story-
board to finished scene.
Embassy guards open
fire on Spawn outside
the Swiss Embassy.

occurred in the Swiss Embassy, when Spawn reveals his amazing and fearsome new abilities. Accomplishing it required elaborate planning and the close collaboration of Croughwell, Dippé, Guillermo Navarro, special effects coordinator Gary Elmendorf, prop master Ron Greenwood, Philip Harrison and Tom Peitzman. The group scouted for the Embassy location, eventually settling on LA's Natural History Museum, and discussed the overall action desired, blocking the moves and figuring how they would interact with each aforementioned department.

Croughwell relied mainly on two stunt doubles for scenes that were too risky to assign to the lead actor, such as a flying leap from balcony to floor.

"Due to the wide range of abilities necessary, William Washington doubled as him for some of the first floor work and Mark Hicks [filled in] for all of the action that required special gymnastic ability," explains Croughwell. "For wider shots that didn't require a good look at the costume, the doubles were utilised. We only used Michael Jai White in close shots. There were a great deal of bullet hits and flying debris, which we coordinated with Gary [Elmendorf] and Ron [Greenwood], so it was safer to use stunt doubles in those situations."

While the Natural History Museum served as the Embassy's interior, an entirely different location doubled as its exterior. The Fine Arts building in downtown Los Angeles provided the Embassy's façade and also the location for another Spawn stunt. Though the Spawn suit's rappelling apparatus and magical cape would be added digitally in post-production, the Spawn stunt double had to physically

scale the building's outer surface, while 'Embassy guards' tried to shoot him down.

Though the alley that Spawn inhabits in the movie was actually a set constructed at Raleigh Studios, it opened up onto a treacherous, teeming boulevard filmed on a downtown street in LA — the new and perilous world that greets Spawn upon his return. The special effects crew added to the omi-

THEY START FIRING AT UPPER WALL

BULLETS
BLAST
AROUND
SPAWN

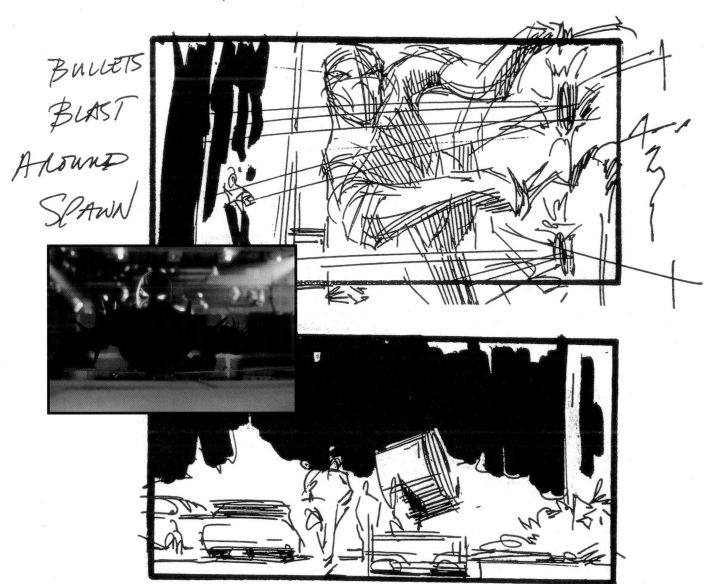

GUARDS RUN TOWARDS AN IDLE
SPOTLIGHT.

132.

Right and opposite: *By the time the chase sequence was shot, the original cement lorry had become a toxic waste truck.*

Below: *Shooting the LA street scenes.*

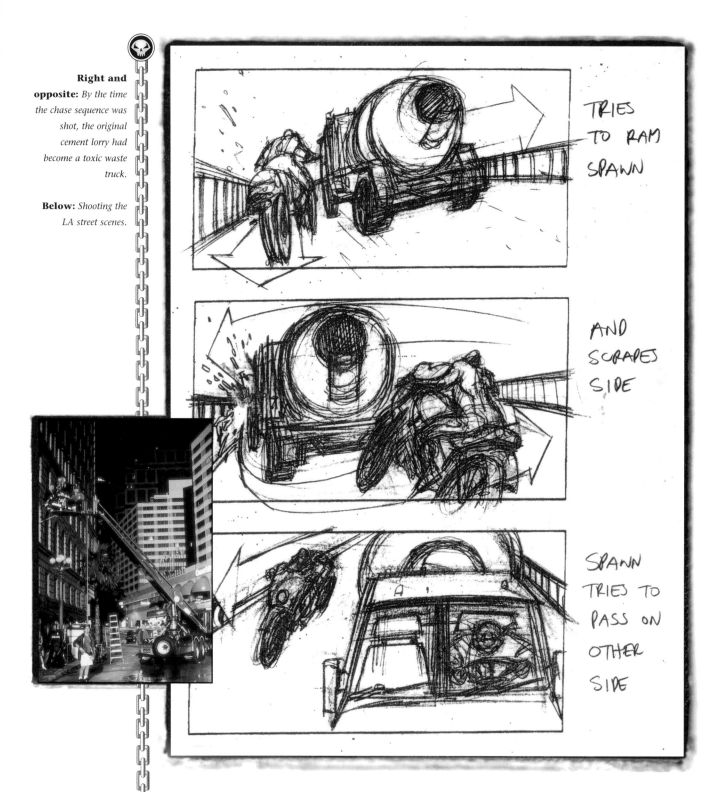

TRIES
TO RAM
SPAWN

AND
SCRAPES
SIDE

SPAWN
TRIES TO
PASS ON
OTHER
SIDE

nous atmosphere by setting up giant rain towers that soaked the hustling extras and underscored the future's inescapable malaise. Ironically, in order to create the particular look this bleak future required, the production team had to clean up the contemporary litter and junk strewn on the street and replace it with 'film filth'.

Both the street and embassy scenes were among several exteriors shot at night, others including the death-defying, high speed motorbike/toxic waste truck chase between Spawn and Clown, and Spawn's graveyard meeting with Clown and some would-be devil worshipping punks. This latter face-to-face encounter with death occurred in an actual cemetery near South Central LA, the cover of night adding sinister, grim undertones to this pivotal sequence.

Right and far right: *'Give me anguish'. Mark Dippé runs through the grave-yard scene with Michael Jai White.*

Below: *A rare, non-sweltering, on set moment for Michael Jai White.*

Once again, an already moody scene was made more poignant still by the addition of digital effects to a locket Spawn retrieves from Simmons' body.

Another night-time location, the site of Simmons' murder — a Korean biological weapons factory — was actually an old refinery in the industrial town of Carson, which the production designers repainted for the movie. The deadly explosion and fire that engulfs Spawn took hours to set up, due to the dangerous materials and specific choreography the scene required. At dawn, the final fires still raged.

Bizarrely, Michael Jai White, who spent most of principal photography sweltering in his rubber Spawn suit, almost froze as the effects technicians prepared to ignite him. The scene involved Jason Wynn spraying Simmons with a "clear, flammable gelatine", and to achieve this, special effects technicians actually swathed White's entire body in a cold gel and lit it. That kind of shot can only be done in one take, and when all the departments were finally ready to film the explosion, the freezing gel had soaked into White's bones.

"By the time they lit me up, I was happy to be on fire, just to get warm," White recalls. "They'd soaked me down with this gel that they kept on ice for four days prior to its application. I don't think I've ever been so cold in my life."

In common with many of the scenes in *Spawn*, some of Martin Sheen's action also necessitated a stunt double, although Croughwell says that "he was ready to do anything that he could." For safety's sake, Croughwell generally relied on stuntman Tom Elliott, although Sheen got his chance to try some

Left: A Carson, California, refinery became the Korean biological weapons factory.

Below: Martin Sheen forsook a stunt double for the film's climactic confrontation.

stunt work, specifically in the scene where Simmons' living room hearth becomes a portal to Hell and Wynn is set ablaze.

"In the house where Wynn is thrown into the fireplace and set on fire, we performed that part with a stunt double, so that Martin could see what was required and the safety measures that would be in place," says Croughwell. "We finished the scene with Martin, setting his back on fire, and he proceeded to roll around on the floor, to give the appearance that he was trying to put himself out. Had it not been for his confidence in us, that we would safely light him on fire, this scene would have lacked a crucial element."

These two sequences would also be incredibly augmented in post-production by computer-generated effects. While Croughwell admits that many members of the stunt community resent the influx of such technology, "... I personally find that by utilising it, I am able to be far more creative with relation to the choreography of all the stunts. There are things that we are able to do now that we could only dream about five years ago and I believe it will only get better from here," Croughwell remarks. "This was a very attractive project to me, in that respect, because I was able to work with people who are at the top of the field, when it comes to CGI. I learned a great deal from them."

VISUAL/ DIGITAL FX

With the main body of special make-up, costume and creature effects established, the computer animation, under the aegis of visual effects supervisor Steve "Spaz" Williams, essentially served as the film's interactive, connective tissue.

Spawn, which features characters who routinely transform from one state to another, as well as two completely antithetical but parallel universes, was a natural candidate for virtual technology. Indeed, the film, which originally featured seventy-seven effects shots, would contain over 300 by its release, each composed of several different elements. To include all the dazzling digital shots, director Dippé and producer Goldman hired fourteen different effects houses, stationed all over the world. Each firm brought different strengths to the film and represented the variety of effects artists that the filmmakers had worked with over the years.

This page: An early computer graphic of the Clown to Violator transformation.

Months in advance of principal photography, Williams laboured at Industrial Light & Magic, constructing the digital versions of Spawn, Clown and the Violator and designing the computer animation for several action sequences and key transformations.

Mark Dippé explains: "What Spaz does, in terms of computer animation, is very similar to traditional stop-motion animation. You take a puppet, you pose it, you take a picture, you pose it a little more... on the computer, he builds a three-dimensional world. He can animate the camera and the model or your character, your digitised actor, and that's what the animation process is. The thing that is so different from stop-motion is that everything is totally fluid. You can place the camera in two positions in space and it will smoothly animate it between the two points."

While Dippé made use of some incredible animatronic puppets, particularly the Violator, the bulk of

its performance would be created in the computer.

"We would use different animatronic Violator puppets for different purposes," Dippé observes. "The main problem with them is that they do not have a full range of motion. You cannot take an animatronic puppet and have it run and leap ten feet. Violator, by the way, was about thirteen feet tall, so we couldn't put a man inside it to effect that kind of movement. A puppet is useful for a very quick, simple motion that can be done in a single shot and lasts a few seconds. That's why we used it, because there were lots of shots of the Violator and we couldn't afford to make them all digital. I would have preferred to, but the cost would have been too

exorbitant. So, we had to mix the two."

Although this powerful, shape-shifting creature really came to life in the computer, the first-unit film team had to shoot the action and actors around it, all of which would be combined in the computer during post-production. This led to some ingenious and comical Violator stand-ins.

"When you are shooting photography for a creature that doesn't exist, the camera is moving and looking for something that is not there," Dippé explains. "So what we would do is make a mock-up. Sometimes it was a head on a stick, sometimes it was a full-scale Violator being moved around by five guys. We'd teach everybody to expect the camera to

go from point A to point B, to understand that one area should be lit because that was where he would be, or, paradoxically, another place should be dark because he would be coming out of it. You'd have to find a way to communicate to everyone, including the actors, where to look, what to do. We had to use a sort of stand-in, even if it was really ridiculous. I mean, I'm sure if the uninitiated came to the set and saw us shooting a Violator sequence with someone holding a head and growling, it would look really stupid, but we had to rehearse with something, use it as a reference and then, when we actually shot, we took it out."

Clint Goldman, a fervent believer in the potential of digital effects, especially in the capable hands of Mark Dippé and Steve Williams, championed the idea of a completely digital Hell:

"Basically, we had to give up seven days of our live-action photography to pay for a digital Hell and I signed my life away, on the dotted line, like Al Simmons."

Goldman's guileless combination of experience, tenacity and zeal paid off. New Line acquiesced, allowing them to take the budget intended for a week of principal photography and convert it into a second-unit shoot, in which the actors performed against blue and green screens. The rest of the money went towards creating this digital Hell.

"Hell didn't exist as a set, there was nothing at all," Goldman explains. "We just shot a wild camera against blue screen. We photographed the actors

against it as much as we could, doing whatever we wanted, totally free and wild. Basically, we took those blue screen elements, incorporated them into the camera move and placed them into different parts of Hell. We moved them around at will in two-dimensional or three-dimensional space, to make them fit into this world that we designed and built."

Opposite: *The Violator in motion.*

Left: *A blue-screen shot is prepared, one that will later be converted into 'digital space'.*

Below: *Virtual Hell, as originally envisaged.*

That world, Goldman promises, will be an epic, visual feat, a Hell nonpareil:

"There have been bits and pieces of what Hell might be in the movies, but in terms of elaborate staging and creation, this is like the *Ben-Hur* of Hells. No one has ever created a digital Hell, as far as I know. Ours is very much a fantasy Hell, with lots of activity and animation. When it's done, it will be very short, maybe only three minutes, but it will be three minutes of pure ecstasy."

Because Hell only existed as a virtual set, the actors had to be digitised to 'perform' in this computerised domain, acting opposite digital creatures. For specific shots, Goldman notes, "... like when they're getting blown up or when they had to be multiplied", the film-makers employed motion capture. This technique 'captured' their movements via electrodes attached to their bodies and logged them into the computer, where they could be manipulated in digital space. Michael Jai White's various postures not only became Spawn's but also created Hell's army. When Spawn kills the expectant horde, it is actually a rendition of Michael Jai White murdering a host of Michael Jai White computerised clones.

This virtual set also required virtual models. In lieu of building a model of the rooftop cathedral, for example, the film-makers created it in the computer. Matte paintings were also digitised. While these computerised tools occasionally had to match the camera angles and lighting established in live-action

shooting, they generally afforded the film-makers a greater flexibility to design and achieve many more shots in a shorter time period than a standard model or matte painting technique would have.

Like the looking-glass universes of the mortal world and Hell that exist in *Spawn*, the digital world in which many of the film's sequences would take place paralleled the physical production. As such, the two separate but equal realms had to match in terms of dimensions, lighting, even camera angle. Dippé explains:

"The way we shot *Spawn*, it was really a live-action and animation combination, and, like all films of this type, we had to find a way to mix and match those elements, especially when we added additional digital shots. Once we created a shot in principal photography, we needed to recreate the same world in the computer. If we shot a plate [location or studio footage over which CGI imagery is added] in which the Violator, which only exists in the computer, is walking into frame and then later, on the computer, I shot the digital Violator with a different lens, when I put the two together it would look weird. The computer lens had to equal the real camera lens, and the digital set had to have the same dimensions. In other words, if I had two walls in the real set and the Violator hit one and then the other, on the computer I had to have the walls in the same place. Otherwise, he'd be hitting air. That process was essential. We had to recreate the real

This page: *The CGI Violator puts the bite on Spawn.*

world in the digital world and marry the two. Then you add your performance, your characters. That's what we're really after, the acting, but we need to reflect the physicality of it in the computer."

Dippé adds that the actor's craft, the indefinable creative process that becomes an indelible performance, is why computer-driven effects will never entirely replace the actor:

"In the course of post-production, we had to put our actors in the computer all the time. In fact, we digitised human beings going through the motions of Spawn, to help us develop the computerised per-

formance. While computer animation allows you to get around the limitation of the physical form, the main problem with it is that it can never cover the expressive range of a human being. A human performance is so amazing, dynamic and adaptable. If we were to replace John Leguizamo or Michael Jai White with computer-animated characters, we never could have achieved the nuances of their portrayals without years and years of work and tons of money. And even then it wouldn't ring true."

Even Williams, whose expertise in computer animation was recently displayed via the digitally enhanced Jabba the Hutt, who appeared in the re-released *Star Wars* trilogy, concurs with Dippé:

"There are so many examples of good computer graphics now, but the challenge is to bring the procedure, which has been wildly overused and abused, back to serve the story. The story is the key element and we used our knowledge of effects to bring it to the screen."

Williams adds that "... this is the first time we've merged every digital technique, every trick we've used in the last eight years. Every tool that is available or has been developed is in *Spawn*, in some shape or another."

Of course, a vital *Spawn* plot point, namely his living, emotive suit, could only be achieved through computer magic. While Michael Jai White wore prosthetic make-up and a remarkable, specially-designed Spawn suit during shooting, which Dippé refers to as "Spawn in the rest-state, when everything is cool and calm," its more active powers were originated digitally.

"One of the essential elements of the comic book that I liked a lot was this living suit, which we called a 'necroplasmic virus'," says Dippé. "It is a living creature that is symbiotically connected to Spawn's body. His body is no longer human, it is this Hellish thing made of 'necroflesh'. One of its principal characteristics is that it is tapped into his nervous system, his mental and emotional state. So, if he gets

This page: *Pre-production sketches of Spawn's 'living suit' and built-in weaponry.*

This page: *Spawn and cape were created entirely in the digital realm and added into the Swiss Embassy scene in post-production.*

angry, it becomes an angry thing. If he tries to grab something, his suit will now enable him to reach it, no matter how far away it is.

"In essence, it is a constantly transforming entity. It doesn't have any fixed shape, it is always mutating, even though it is effectively his armour. Because it is continually changing, it can be created very naturally by digital techniques. To me, it is very similar to the water snake in *The Abyss* or the liquid-metal man in *T2*, except that it is not as abstract. It is a human element, with the quality of a 'second skin.' Basically, we had to really create a living being."

The cache of weapons built into Spawn's armour, including a mutable cape, retractable talons and a protective mask, also came under the aegis of computer animation.

"The cape has many powers, but is essentially defensive and predatory," Dippé continues. "It's like those insects that have weird, double-eyes on their wings... the cape has the potential to instil fear in others and, like the whole suit, it also reflects Spawn's fear. It can become massive and formidable, while simultaneously protecting Spawn, like a shield. Another feature of his armour is that he can grow spikes and blades. So, if a hand grabs him from behind on the shoulder, the shoulder spouts spikes that will pierce the hand. It also features a mask that can cover and uncover his face, to allow him to be more human-like when he needs to be more meditative. So, all of these transforming things, we couldn't accomplish them in a practical sense, you can't make a suit that does all that."

While it was clear that the computer would create

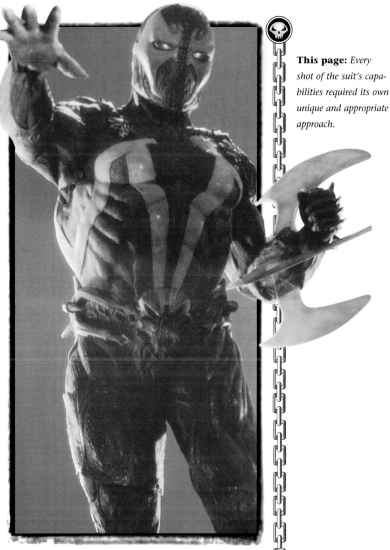

This page: *Every shot of the suit's capabilities required its own unique and appropriate approach.*

the more "animated" aspects of the suit, every shot still required its own unique and appropriate approach.

"The game with visual effects is like film-making in general," Dippé observes. "There are a million different ways to accomplish a shot... sometimes you use a dolly, sometimes you use a Steadicam, sometimes you put the actor on a dolly and move him around. The trick is to find the right means to the desired end. For instance, the mask rising up over Spawn's face: once, we shot Michael without the mask and then shot him wearing it and we'd go between, but, generally, we'd film Michael without the mask and have him do this angry reaction and then the mask would be digitally added over his face."

Goldman muses that by the time *Spawn* opens "... our post-production budget will be as much as our production budget. We only shot principal photography for sixty-three days. We'll use a great percentage of what we shot, but we knew the bulk of the movie would really be made in post-[production]." ☠

SOUNDTRACK

Composer Graeme Revell's innovative musical arrangements have graced such films as Wim Wenders' moody *Until the End of the World*, the riveting horror-thriller *The Crow*, Kathryn Bigelow's unsettling virtual reality drama *Strange Days* and Phillip Noyce's action thriller *The Saint*. Revell earned his musical credentials during the late seventies, founding the influential industrial band SPK, which pioneered the use of metal percussion, chant and sound design.

"We sold our records ourselves, through word-of-mouth and letter writing," Revell recalls. "In many ways, that underground audience that found us is

Right: *Composer Graeme Revell.*

similar to the one that embraces the comic book world. It's related to the same subversive energy."

It was this audience that Revell constantly considered when scoring *Spawn*: "The first thing in my mind was the audience. There's a language of music that this audience appreciates which involves the relationship between the movie score and songs. I wanted the music to be a unified whole that was comprised of both."

Revell sampled a variety of works and artists, introducing new bands in combination with better known groups, creating intriguing and incongruous matches, such as songs from the band Orbital performed by the guitarist from Metallica.

"I wanted the music to take chances and I thought I could do that with these new, underground bands," explains Revell. "I love to give young bands the opportunity to do something like this. We'll be introducing a new group called Plug through *Spawn*. Basically, I tried to find an emerging techno band and combined their songs with an established rock group, providing separate units of music for each scene. I didn't want the score to stray into big orchestral numbers. I didn't think that was the spirit of *Spawn*."

Revell, who read the comic book for several years prior to his affiliation with the movie, felt that the film required music that would be "... completely new, very strong, energetic, hard and percussive. After all, it's about the ultimate battle for the world."

The film-makers' vision of the comic book's cine-matic avatar attracted Revell to the project:

"I certainly appreciated the technical *tour de force* it would be, given the visual nature of the book and the film team connected to the movie. I was very inspired by Mark and Clint's previous work and found them to be very forward thinking in their approach to everything in the movie, including the music."

The film's amazing visual effects provided Revell with his greatest challenge, however.

"The different effects were coming in bit-by-bit in post-production, as I was scoring the film," Revell remembers. "Sometimes, after seeing the effects added to the scene, I would alter my early versions of the music, refining and cutting as they came in, to fit the visual flavour of the scene."

New Zealand-born Revell found his way into movie music via Australian director George Miller and the darkly comedic, futuristic movie *Mad Max*: "I was sitting in my [music] publisher's office and overheard him talking to George Miller, who wanted some hip-hop music for *Mad Max*. I figured I could do that in five minutes. Well, it took an hour and five minutes and I made $3,000. I thought that was an incredible hourly rate!"

His musical skill and reputation led him to score his first film, for another Australian director, Phillip Noyce. The movie was the edgy thriller *Dead Calm*, starring Nicole Kidman, and, along with his audacious work on *Mad Max*, it established Revell as a cutting-edge film composer and music supervisor.

Below: *The film's many special visual effects, added in post-production, meant Revell often revised his original score.*

SPAWN®

The Cast

Clown	John Leguizamo
Al Simmons/Spawn	Michael Jai White
Jason Wynn	Martin Sheen
Wanda	Theresa Randle
Cogliostro	Nicol Williamson
Terry Fitzgerald	D.B. Sweeney
Zack Webb	Miko Hughes
Cyan	Sydney Beaudoin
Jessica Priest	Melinda Clarke

The Film-makers

Music by	Graeme Revell
Creature, Costume and Make-up Effects by	Kurtzman, Nicotero & Berger EFX Group, Inc.
Special Animation and Visual Effects by	Industrial Light & Magic
Edited by	Michael N. Knue, A.C.E.
Production Designer	Philip Harrison
Director of Photography	Guillermo Navarro
Co-Executive Producers	Brian Witten & Adrianna Aj Cojen
Visual Effects Supervisor	Steve "Spaz" Williams
Associate Producer	Terry Fitzgerald
Executive Producers	Todd McFarlane & Alan C. Blomquist
Screenplay by	Alan McElroy
Produced by	Clint Goldman
Directed by	Mark A.Z. Dippé

SPAWN®

COLLECTIONS FROM TITAN BOOKS